# RUN FAST

# RUN FAST

## How to Train For a 5-K or 10-K Race

By Hal Higdon,
Senior Writer, **RUNNER'S** *WORLD* Magazine

Copyright © 1992 by Hal Higdon Communications, Inc.

Printed in the United States of America on acid-free paper ⊗

"Ten Tips on Running Form" on pages 62 and 63 is adapted from *The
Complete Canadian Runner* by Fred Wilt. Reprinted with permission
from the author.

Book Editor: Kathleen A. Becker
Book and Cover Designer: Lynn N. Gano
Cover Photographer: John Kelly
Copy Editor: Susan G. Berg

If you have any questions or comments concerning this book, please
write:
   Rodale Press
   Book Reader Service
   33 East Minor Street
   Emmaus, PA 18098

**Library of Congress Cataloging-in-Publication Data**
Higdon, Hal
   Run fast : how to train for a 5-K or 10-K race / by Hal Higdon.
      p.     cm.
   Includes bibliographical references and index.
   ISBN 0–87596–103–7 paperback
   1. Running—Training.     I. Title.
GV1061.5.H54   1992
796.42—dc20                                              91–42426
                                                            CIP


**Distributed in the book trade by St. Martin's Press**

   4  6  8  10  9  7  5        paperback

To Emil Zatopek, the 1948 and 1952 Olympic champion.
I once saw the great Czechoslovakian runner win a
5000-meter race at a track meet in West Germany. That
memory continues to inspire me. All runners who seek to
run fast follow in Zatopek's footsteps.

# CONTENTS

# INTRODUCTION

Before the start of the Honolulu Marathon, I encountered Frank Shorter, whose victory in the Olympic marathon at Munich is credited with launching the running boom. Shorter still competes, but with less intensity than in 1972, when he also placed fifth in the Olympic 10,000 meters.

"How's your running, Frank?" I asked, offering a conversational gambit.

"I'm in good shape," Shorter replied. "I'm just slow."

It's not just Frank Shorter. Improving speed is a concern for all of us. We want to run fast, particularly in the popular short distances—the 5-K and 10-K.

"That's the first question runners ask at clinics," says Olympian Francie Larrieu Smith. "They want to know 'How can I run faster?'"

Good question. While numerous books have told people how to start jogging and how to finish their first marathon, less attention is paid to running short races faster. Many of the millions of participants in the current fitness boom skipped high school track and cross-country, where they might have learned the necessary skills. They didn't run in college, either. As a result, they missed the training you get at that level. They never learned to warm up properly. They don't have a coach. They don't know about interval training, fartlek, and bounding drills. "They haven't learned how to train for speed," explains Robert Vaughan, Larrieu Smith's coach.

While researching this book, I spoke with numerous world-class athletes and their coaches. Talented and well trained, these fast athletes often felt the answer to my question about improving speed was almost too simple. More than one told me: "To run fast, you simply run fast." That includes Lynn Jennings, 1990 and 1991 world cross-country champion. Jennings said: "The trick to running fast is to make sure you run fast in training. Just covering the mileage won't do the job." Keith Brantly, one of America's top track runners, agreed, adding: "You have to drill your body to run fast."

Jennings and Brantly instinctively know the type of training required to reach peak performance. From years spent as competitive athletes, they also understand that achieving top speed in a specific race requires more than a few fast workouts. It requires a base of endurance before beginning those workouts. It requires planning and organization and a knowledge of other disciplines, from diet to flexibility to tactics. It also requires a lot of trial and error, realizing that what works for others in training may not necessarily work for you—and vice versa. It requires body knowledge and body sensitivity, and even with all that in place, you may need the assistance of a good coach.

During a long running career, I worked with numerous coaches—some more knowledgeable than others—and I learned something new from each. As a sophomore at U-High in Chicago, I went out for Paul Derr's track team and learned that I had talent, running 5:04 for the mile. I transferred to a new school my junior year and missed a season. As a senior under the supervision of Mike O'Connor at Chicago's Mount Carmel High School, I learned talent was not enough, since I failed to match my earlier time.

At Carleton College in Northfield, Minnesota, I learned about overdistance and underdistance from cross-country coach Cy DeCoster. My track coach, Wally Haas, introduced me to repeats. With that as key to my training, I won conference titles in the mile and half-mile.

Attending graduate school at the University of Chicago, I came under the influence of Ted Haydon, a master motivator. What he lacked in technical knowledge he more than made up for through his ability to provide an environment that allowed for different training styles and personalities. Under Haydon's guidance, I increased my mileage and placed high in several national championships.

Later, the United States Army sent me overseas to Germany, where my coach was Frank McBride, a 1500-meter finalist at the 1952 Olympic Trials. The rage then was interval training, which helped me slice a full minute off my best time for 5000 meters. Returning from the service, I placed fifth at the 1960 Olympic Trials in the 3000-meter steeplechase.

Eventually, I put my fate in the hands of Fred Wilt, a national-champion distance runner and FBI agent who later coached at Purdue University. He taught me how to blend distance and speed. Under his guidance, I placed fifth at the 1964 Boston Marathon, the first American to cross the line. Not bad, I thought, for someone who didn't have enough speed to break five minutes for the mile in high school.

During my long career, I had the opportunity to visit the laboratories of the eminent exercise physiologists and physicians David L. Costill, Ph.D., Michael L. Pollock, Ph.D., and Kenneth H. Cooper, M.D. They tested me on treadmills to increase their own knowledge, but I also usually went home a wiser runner.

Once past the age of 40, I achieved more success as a masters runner, setting numerous records while winning world and national titles.

As a senior writer for *Runner's World,* I have shared this information with millions of readers who run. In that position, I have had the opportunity to meet and interview many of the world's most knowledgeable coaches, from Percy Cerutty to Arthur Lydiard, from Bill Bowerman to Jack Daniels, Ph.D. Although their techniques differ, these coaches share a basic ability to motivate athletes. They also know how to teach athletes—some of them gifted, some of them less gifted—to run fast.

This book, finally, is a compilation of what I learned from them and what I learned from myself.

# Chapter 1

# QUICK STRIDES

## THE THRILL OF THE SHORT RUN

**T**he running world has quick-ened its stride. The new motto for those who fueled the fitness boom is: Run Short, Run Fast! Runners are looking for variety in their racing, and short distances are catching their fancy. They also are intrigued by the challenge of training like track athletes.

And so runners of every caliber are gearing up for the short distances that pack a punch—the 5-K and the 10-K. In 1990, according to Basil and Linda Honikman of TACSTATS (the official record-keeper for American road races), 1.2 million runners participated in 10-K races, more than in any other event. And it continues to be the most popular race today. The largest 10-K is Atlanta's Peachtree Road Race. Approximately 40,000 run in that race alone.

Running at the heels of its bigger sibling, the 5-K has jumped, since 1983, from eighth to second in popularity among race distances. This shorter—although not necessarily gentler—event attracted 583,000 finishers in 1990, an increase of about 11.7 percent over the year before. At the 1989 World Veterans Championships in Eugene, Oregon, so many masters ran the 5-K that organizers needed 38 heats!

While the 10-K retains its popularity as the most favored road race, another frequent distance is the 8-K—third most popular, with 361,000 finishers. (Fourth on the TACSTATS list is the marathon, with 263,000 finishers.)

Why is the 10-K so popular? For one thing, 10,000 meters is the longest standard event in track competition; when transferred to the road, therefore, it becomes a convenient measure of performance—like the mile. The 10-K also has more status than many other road events because like the 5-K, it is an Olympic distance. And on days that are hot and humid, the 10-K proves to be a relatively safe race distance, since even a moderately trained runner can finish in an hour; faster runners squeeze in under 30 minutes.

Organizers interested in attracting large numbers of participants often schedule the 10-K, since it is a distance easily covered by the average jogger. But elite runners enjoy the short distance, too. Craig Virgin, a two-time world cross-country champion, agrees. He explains: "Most runners who specialize in the marathon are lucky to run two or three quality races at that distance a year. I might be able to run that many 10-K road races in a month without suffering similar stress."

Certainly that is one reason why runners increasingly have become attracted to shorter distances: less stress. But stress is not necessarily all bad, because it can help you become a faster runner. According to Bob Glover, director of the New York Road Runners Club's coaching program: "Many runners, especially beginning racers, underestimate their abilities as athletes. Through speed training, they often discover that they are tougher than they had realized."

# YOUR FIRST STEP TO A FASTER PACE

To run fast, first make running fun. Mostly as a hobby, because I enjoy it, I coach the cross-country teams—boys and girls—at Elston High School in Michigan City, Indiana. Our season lasts from August through October. It's a period of intense training, with races twice weekly, Tuesdays and Saturdays. Studies suffer. It's not always fun, although winning can be fun.

But at season's end, we relax and return to basics: low-pressure running designed to recharge our batteries. Each November, I appear at school several days a week to run with those team members who want to stay in shape for track. For fun as much as for fitness, we'll run trails through some scenic area nearby. It's just a frolic in the woods. A half dozen or more students will show.

One day, two new girls appeared: one, a sophomore named Daniella; the other, a freshman named Carla. Carla had participated in volleyball that fall and thus had attained at least some level of endurance; Daniella, on the other hand, was new to athletics. Since both girls planned to run track in the spring, Benny Edwards, their track coach, had suggested they join us.

Okay, but I didn't feel like doing much coaching that day. I just wanted to enjoy the workout. We ran on trails near the Bailly Homestead in the Indiana Dunes National Lakeshore. It was late afternoon. We could see the setting sun through trees stripped of leaves.

I suspected Daniella and Carla might have difficulty matching the pace of our regulars. We were heading out on an out-and-back route, so I told them to follow at whatever pace they wanted and to do a U-turn as soon as they spotted us coming back.

We went off whooping and hollering and having a good time on the winding trail. It had recently rained heavily, so there was standing water in places. We zigzagged back and forth between the obstacles, shouting "Water!" or

"Root!" to warn those behind us of hazards underfoot, probably scaring every deer within 3 miles. "Snake!" I yelled to panic Liz, the girls' captain—except she was used to hearing it and stopped paying attention to me. (Some day we'll encounter a real snake; then Liz will be sorry.)

We raced down a gully and across a boardwalk nearly engulfed by a flooding stream. "White water!" someone shouted. We were spread out over a quarter-mile of trail, and the woods reverberated with our foolishness. Tony, the boys' team captain, rushed ahead with one or two others, and it was a while before I could catch up with them and turn them around. I glanced at my watch. We had been running 30 minutes, which meant that our total workout was going to be close to an hour. Meanwhile, I forgot all about my two beginning runners. Benny's going to kill me, I thought.

I encountered Daniella and Carla coming back and slowed to observe their progress. Hmmmm, I thought, they're doing all right. Carla was further ahead, but she may have turned back earlier. Daniella was walking, and I worried that we might be waiting a long time for her to finish. But we came to a downhill and she ran down it, then walked up the other side, then started running again. I offered a word of encouragement as I passed and positioned myself between the two girls to make certain they didn't miss any turns. When they got back to the parking lot—tired, but not totally destroyed—everybody gave them a big cheer. When I got back to school, I'd tell Benny they would make fine runners. Sometimes the best coaching you do is no coaching.

## PEDDLING MOTIVATION

Consider for a moment the beginners like Carla and Daniella, who have not yet even run their first 10-K, much less begun to worry about running it faster. The best advice anyone can offer a beginner is: Just do it! Begin like Carla

and Daniella did. Walk and jog without anybody looking over your shoulder.

Beginners occupy a unique—and fortunate—position in the running world, because every move is upward. "One of the joys of being a beginning runner is that you continue to get better," says Mary Reed, a coach with the Atlanta Track Club. "Everything is improvement until you reach that first plateau. It's an innocent time of joy in any runner's life that a lot of us would like to go back to."

One winter night a dozen years ago, I was changing in the locker room of our local racquet club when a tennis enthusiast inquired about the group of people that surrounded me. "What are you doing?" he asked.

I explained about the beginning running class I was then teaching with my wife, Rose, and that we met once a week to run together around the racquet club's indoor track.

The tennis player seemed surprised: "I didn't know you could teach running."

He was right, of course. You don't need to teach running—or shouldn't need to. Children learn to run almost as soon as they learn to walk. Visit any elementary school playground, and you'll see kids running all over the place. An athlete who goes out for any sport in high school—football, basketball, tennis—runs as part of the conditioning for that sport, or should! It is only as adults that people forget to run and sometimes have to be taught again.

Running is basically a simple movement. To quote 1976 Olympic marathoner and *Runner's World* senior writer Don Kardong: "First you put your right foot forward. Then you put your left foot forward. Then you do it again." It's that simple.

When Rose and I teach people to run, we try to get them to start slowly. Some beginners (particularly if they're overweight) need to walk first, beginning with a half hour, three or four days a week. Then we suggest that they jog a short distance until they get slightly out of breath, walk to recover, then jog some more. Jog, walk. Jog, walk. After a while, they achieve an ability to run a mile without stopping. (Interestingly, the jog-walk-jog-walk approach used

by beginners mimics interval training, a very sophisticated method for improving performance. I'll cover interval training in detail in chapter 8.)

We preach moderation, following the motto coined by New Zealand coach Arthur Lydiard: Train, don't strain. We also talk about efficient running form, diet, equipment, safety, and avoiding injuries, and every now and then we show a film featuring some running guru, such as Ken Cooper, M.D., or George Sheehan, M.D.

But mostly, we are not teaching running; rather, we're *peddling motivation.* We realize it takes courage to don a pair of running shoes and step out on a sidewalk for the first time, in front of friends and neighbors. Quite honestly, a lot of beginning runners never get moving out of fear of looking foolish. They lack self-confidence. They fear failure.

One advantage of a class situation, of course, is the group support you get from others of equal ability. The most important thing we tell beginners is not how to hold their arms or how far to jog without stopping, but simply "You're looking good. You're doing great. Keep it up." Basic motivation. Natural running instincts, developed in childhood, simply take over.

Meet Bette Murray. She worked in the computer center at Purdue University–North Central. Her motivation was simple: She wanted to lose a few pounds.

Murray started slowly in our class at the racquet club. We had her walk and encouraged her to do a little more each week. Finally one evening, she set out after her goal: to run 16 laps—1 mile—around the club's track without stopping.

When she completed her 16th lap, she was more exultant than tired. "I never believed I could do it," she said.

Of course, Rose and I knew she could do it. She didn't need us to teach her to run; we simply supplied a little motivation. Murray never did compete in the Boston Marathon, and I haven't seen her in any 10-K races recently, but she did experience a victory. She reached her goal of running 1 mile. To some people, that may sound like a small achievement, but as Murray's motivators, we were very proud.

Finding a good class is an important first step. You're more likely to find running classes offered in the spring, a time when warm weather beckons people outdoors. I teach an annual spring fitness class at a hospital in my hometown. It's mostly for walkers, but runners also join us. To find similar classes in your area, check with hospitals or fitness clubs. Community colleges, such as Southwestern Michigan College near me, often offer classes in fitness, walking, jogging, and even marathon running. Running clubs usually welcome beginning joggers. Some, such as the Atlanta Track Club, offer personalized coaching. To locate a running club in your area, contact the Road Runners Club of America, 629 South Washington Street, Alexandria, VA 22314; (703) 836-0558.

# *YOUR FIRST TIME AT THE STARTING LINE*

Sooner or later, most runners want to test their new-found fitness in a race, typically a 5-K or a 10-K. Not much serious training is required to finish these distances: perhaps three or four workouts a week over a period of several months. Running an average of a dozen miles a week will do the trick. That does not mean you will finish the race comfortably, or near the front, but you *will* finish.

And you need *not* run the full race distance during a workout to prove you can do it in competition. Most marathoners, for instance, run no farther than 20 miles in a climactic long workout before attempting a 26-mile race.

If you can cover 4 miles in practice several times over a period of weeks, without excessive straining, the spirit of the moment should carry you across the finish line of a 10-K—as long as you start slowly and keep a steady pace. (Reaching a 5-K finish line requires slightly less training mileage.)

Once you've finished your first race, however, you will find that a new goal beckons. You'll realize that it no longer is enough for you to merely cover the distance; you will want to cover it progressively faster. You will enter the

## TRAINING UP FOR YOUR FIRST RACE

Here is a simple, eight-week training schedule designed to get you ready for a short-distance road race. For this workout program, we assume that you have no serious health problems, are not grossly overweight, are in reasonably good physical condition, and have already done some light jogging. If not, gradually build up a fitness base, first with walking and then with jogging. For safety's sake, you probably should obtain an exercise stress test from a qualified cardiologist or physiologist.

The following program is designed for runners preparing for a 10-K. If your goal distance is shorter, you can modify the program by using *slightly* shorter training distances, particularly for your Sunday "long" runs.

**Weeks 1 and 2 (6 miles each week)**
**Sunday:** 1- to 2-mile run, steady
**Monday:** rest
**Tuesday:** 1-mile jog
**Wednesday:** some light walking
**Thursday:** 2 miles, jogging and walking
**Friday:** 1-mile jog
**Saturday:** some light walking

**Weeks 3 and 4 (9 miles each week)**
**Sunday:** 2- to 3-mile run, steady
**Monday:** rest

world of *performance,* replete with training logs, featherweight racing shoes, and inside expertise to shave seconds from your PR.

The term *PR* is part of the running jargon; it means personal record. Few of us will ever set a world or national record, but *anybody* can establish a PR. Any time you've

**Tuesday:** 2 miles, jogging and walking
**Wednesday:** 1-mile jog
**Thursday:** 2 miles, steady
**Friday:** 1-mile jog
**Saturday:** some light walking


**Weeks 5 and 6 (12 miles each week)**
**Sunday:** 3- to 4-mile run, steady
**Monday:** rest
**Tuesday:** 2-mile jog
**Wednesday:** 1-mile jog
**Thursday:** 3 miles, jogging and walking
**Friday:** 2-mile jog
**Saturday:** some light walking and jogging


**Weeks 7 and 8 (15 miles each week)**
**Sunday:** 4-mile run, steady
**Monday:** rest
**Tuesday:** 3 miles, jogging and walking
**Wednesday:** 2-mile jog
**Thursday:** 3 miles, steady
**Friday:** 2-mile jog
**Saturday:** 1-mile jog

Take a day or two off before you run your first 10-K to make certain you are well rested. And take another day or two off afterward. You will have earned it.

recorded over a distance (even odd distances in training) becomes your PR. Every time you run that course or distance, you will have an opportunity to better that PR.

As you become more involved in improving your performances, keep in mind that setting new PRs may not always be easy—or advisable. To improve, runners gradually increase their training mileage. Eventually, however, they move away from that time of joy described by coach Mary Reed and find themselves upon difficult plateaus, where they are faced with the worry of training too little or too much.

Jack Daniels, Ph.D., an exercise physiologist and coach at the State University of New York at Cortland, writes: "Almost anyone can stay happy and injury-free simply by jogging a couple of miles a day. Fine. But these same runners would be even happier if they could run faster. That's simply human nature. We want to get better, and that brings us face-to-face with the quintessential training question: How can you train hard enough to improve, but not so hard that you get burned out and/or injured?"

But first things first. To establish your PR, of course, you'll need to run the course. Follow the plans in "Training Up for Your First Race" on page 8 to get started. If you've already run a 5-K or 10-K and you're eager to work on increasing your speed, move on to chapter 2 to learn how to begin this process.

# Chapter 2

# THE SECRET OF SUCCESS

## START SLOW TO FINISH FAST

On a crisp winter morning, I rose early while staying at a hotel near Arlington Park, a racetrack northwest of Chicago, and went for a slow run on the bike paths of nearby Busse Woods. As I encountered other joggers, walkers, and cyclists, I greeted them with a nod or brief hello.

Two of the joggers apparently recognized me. I heard one say to the other after I passed: "What's he doing out here?"

I was not there to bet on the horses, since the track was closed for the season. Actually, I was on my way home from a track meet in Madison, Wisconsin. I stopped with my wife, Rose, to attend a wedding reception at the Arlington Park Hilton, which usually caters to horse fans. As to why I was in that particular forest preserve early on a Sunday morning, I was doing some base training to get in shape for the speedwork I planned for later that spring. I might have replied to the pair: "I'm legging myself up."

That's an expression used by horse people. Ed Benham, a retired jockey from Ocean City, Maryland, who has set nearly 100 American track and road records for runners age 70 and older, taught it to me.

# LESSONS FROM A TRACK OF ANOTHER SORT

Horses move pretty quickly, so what's good enough for a horse is good enough for me. While legging it up, I was moving at a pace *so* slow as to bore even most beginners. During a 90-minute run near the racetrack that morning, I covered 9 or 10 miles. That's barely a 10-minute-mile pace. Run that slow in most 10-K races, and you'll finish in the bottom 10 percent of the field. But that's part of Benham's method. He obviously runs decidedly faster when he races.

As pedestrian as they may seem, those slow miles near the racetrack would result in fast finishes later during the year. Certainly my performance earlier in Madison indicated that I needed a good shot of speed. In the 1500 meters, the top two runners left me after one lap. I paced the rest of the field for five more laps. Then three runners swept past me on the last circuit.

After that defeat, the logical training response would seem to be to run sprints to improve my finishing kick— perhaps some lung-searing sessions of 400-meter sprints on the track. You can't run fast unless you train fast, everyone says.

True, if your sprints are done at the right time of the year. But another adage says that you can't run fast unless you first train *slow*. Ron Gunn, track coach at Southwestern Michigan College, puts it this way: "You can't shoot a cannon out of a canoe." The cannon's recoil, of course, would pitch both the cannon and the person firing it into the water. You need a bigger base—like a battleship—for cannons. And runners who expect to go fast in competition need a better base than what they can obtain with speed-work alone.

Thus, those slow miles in the woods near Arlington Park were designed to *prepare* me to run fast.

Benham learned that on the job. He rode his first race as a jockey at Culver City, California, at age 14. Two years later, he scored his first victory. Benham rode competitively until 1940, then worked as an outrider and equipment handler until he retired in 1976.

Soon afterward, Benham started to run with his two sons and achieved instant success as an age-group competitor. "I trained myself just like I trained the horses," says Benham.

That meant starting slow. Or as Benham describes the base training he used to give horses: "You leg them up." For six to eight weeks, the horses would gallop very slowly. Finally, Benham would throw in a little speed, "breezing them," as they say at the track. He would run the horses, first ⅛ mile, then ¼ mile, until they worked up to ⅝ mile fast. If the horses seemed tired, he would back off on the hard training one or two days, walking them around the shed for an hour each day until they recovered their pep.

"One way you could tell if a racehorse was overtrained," says Benham, "was that the horse wouldn't finish his feed." Loss of appetite is a symptom of overtraining among runners, too, although sometimes we are less likely to react with rest, unless we have a coach or trainer advising us.

Other warning signs for overtrained runners are restlessness at night, a slightly elevated pulse rate just before rising, or dead legs and a general feeling of fatigue. Race times suffer, too. You're likely to catch colds because of lowered resistance. A certain amount of muscle soreness and stiffness is a natural part of the training process, but if symptoms of fatigue persist for more than two or three days, don't take an aspirin or see a doctor as you might for that cold. The best advice is simply to cut mileage until, like Benham's horses, you recover your pep.

When Benham turned to running at the age of 71, his approach to his new sport was similar to the way he had approached his horse racing. "Nobody told me how to run," he says, "so I legged myself up first. Once I got into shape, then I stretched out." Benham means he cut his training distance and increased the speed of his runs, thus stretching his stride.

# RUN LONG TO RUN FAST

For any running machine—human or horse—success depends on the development of a strong aerobic base: endurance. It is the foundation of your running performance. "Endurance training must come first," insists Bill Dellinger, track coach at the University of Oregon. "Speed is merely a supplement to strength."

So how do you develop endurance? With the long run. Benji Durden, a 1980 Olympic marathoner and now a coach in Boulder, Colorado, says: "One thing I strongly believe in is the value of a long run. A lot of people, when trying to run fast, overlook the need for strength. There's great value in the weekly long run. If you're pointing for a short race, you still need to run long in training. Just because you're not running over 2 hours in a race, that doesn't mean that runs that long have no value in your training program."

New Zealand's Peter Snell demonstrated the value of a sound aerobic base when he won the 800 meters at the 1960 Olympics, then again at the 1964 Olympics, when he also won the 1500 meters. At the end of his career, Snell moved to the United States and obtained a doctorate in exercise physiology. He now directs the St. Paul Human Performance Center, connected with the University of Texas Southwestern Medical Center in Dallas, Texas. "My best seasons came on top of my best buildups," recalls Snell, who trained under the supervision of renowned coach Arthur

Lydiard. In 1961, Lydiard and Snell returned from a summer of racing on the European track circuit and spent four months running long, slow distance. (Joe Henderson, writer and editor for *Runner's World,* later would coin the phrase *L.S.D.* to describe that type of training.) "Slow" for Snell meant 7-minute miles. Toward the end of 1961, he was averaging more than 100 miles a week in his training, including a long run over one of Lydiard's favorite 22-mile courses. Snell entered one marathon in December and finished at 2:41:00. Several weeks later, he ran a 4:01.5 mile during a handicap race held at a carnival on New Year's Day.

"The time startled me," Snell recalls, "because I didn't start my speedwork until after the marathon. That convinced me of the value of the Lydiard three-month buildup." Within the next month, Snell ran a 3:54.4 mile and a 1:44.3 800 meters. Today, 30 years later, those performances would still win many major track competitions.

How could L.S.D. training prepare an athlete to run so fast? As an exercise physiologist, Snell believes that developing an aerobic base is the one essential first step. "It permits you to do more race-related training once you finally do shift to speedwork."

## FINDING SPEED
## IN THE LONG RUN

Snell believes another benefit of L.S.D. training was the development of his faster muscles. Interestingly, it was the *end* of his long runs that benefited his speed the most. Snell described running his first 22-miler in company with Murray Halberg, winner of the 5000 meters at the 1960 Olympics. Fifteen miles into the workout, Snell began to feel fatigued and thought he might stop and get a ride to the finish.

"Do that and you'll totally waste the workout," said Halberg. "The value begins at 15 miles."

Now, as an exercise physiologist, Snell understands why. It relates to the training of the two basic types of muscle

fibers: fast-twitch and slow-twitch. Sprinters have a preponderance of the first; distance runners, the second. It is
one reason they have success in their respective events.

During the first portion of the long, slow run, the body
gradually depletes its supply of glycogen in the slow-twitch
muscles. Once that supply is depleted, Snell claims, the
body must turn to the fast-twitch muscles to continue to
run efficiently. Thus, toward the end of L.S.D. training,
those muscles so essential for speed also are exercised.

Soviet coach A. Yakimov explains: "At first it was thought
that long continuous running helped perfect only the aerobic processes, but specialists have since come to the conclu-
sion that it also helps develop the anaerobic potentials of
the runner." Yakimov advises that coaches (and runners)
must be very careful in selecting both the speed and duration of the run. Yakimov wrote in *Track Technique:* "The
problem is that the athlete must be able to distribute his
effort in order to run the whole way at an even pace. If the
pace drops off at the end, the problem has not been solved."

In other words, a workout that starts fast and finishes
slow may fail to train the fast-twitch muscles properly.

But a danger exists if runners train only with long runs.
They eventually develop the gait and the rhythm of the
long-distance runner. They become efficient at running
slowly for a long period of time. Their strides may change,
and they lose their speed. They no longer can run fast at
shorter distances in an efficient way.

"The major disadvantage of concentrating on 'volume' in
training is that long, slow distance training is considerably
slower than racing pace," according to David L. Costill,
Ph.D., director of the Human Performance Laboratory at
Ball State University. "Such training fails to develop the
neurological patterns of muscle fiber recruitment that will
be needed during races that require a faster pace. Since the
selective use of muscle fibers differs according to running
speed, runners who train only at speeds slower than
race pace will not train all of the muscle fibers needed for
competition."

The best method for developing speed, therefore, is to

begin with a slow aerobic base, then move to the fast anaerobic training.

## *THE HEART OF THE MATTER*

To run fast, you must have a cardiovascular system capable of efficient oxygen delivery. Within certain limits, the more oxygen your muscles receive, the faster you can run. Scientists don't entirely understand the reasons, but an efficient oxygen delivery system—aerobic base—is best developed by training within 70 to 85 percent of your *maximum heart rate (MHR)*.

When an athlete moves beyond 85 percent of his MHR, he crosses his *anaerobic threshold*, or *lactate threshold*, with different physiological effects (as I'll cover in chapter 11). By training anaerobically, you can develop your muscular system's ability to readily *release* energy from your muscles. But you must possess a solid aerobic base first. If you don't, you won't be able to deliver oxygen to your muscles, and your performances will diminish.

Robert H. Vaughan, a coach whose best-known athlete is world-class distance runner Francie Larrieu Smith, described this in the dissertation he wrote to obtain his doctorate at the University of North Texas. Vaughan noticed that some of the athletes he coached were more capable than others of maintaining their competitive ability over a longer period of time. One was Larrieu Smith, who set personal records at the 1988 Olympic Trials in July, then ran still faster at the Games in September, where she placed fifth in the 10,000 meters.

Looking back on Larrieu Smith's training, Vaughan realized that one key to her consistency was that she had maintained her aerobic base by running regular 20-mile workouts, even while preparing for a race one-tenth that distance. Larrieu Smith was training for seemingly selfish reasons, though. Not only was she primed for the Olympics, she also was looking five weeks beyond the Games to running in the Columbus Marathon. Theoretically, training for this marathon could have had a negative effect on Larrieu

*(continued on page 21)*

# BUILDING AN AEROBIC BASE

Following is a basic 12-week training schedule designed to build your aerobic base, which is necessary before you can begin speedwork, a more demanding type of training. The aerobic base program is an extension of the program designed to prepare runners for their first race, which was outlined at the end of chapter 1.

But don't skip immediately from that program, with its maximum weekly mileage of 15, to this, with its start at 20 miles. Instead, consolidate your gains by holding to a weekly total of 15 to 20 miles for at least another 8 to 12 weeks, if not longer. Run a few more road races at distances between 5-K and 10-K. Enjoy the fun of being a new runner. After your times have begun to plateau—or after the race season ends—then it is time to seek further improvement by ceasing to race long enough to build your aerobic base.

In fact, for the following program to work *best,* four factors probably should be present: (1) You have been running at least for several years; (2) you can run 20 to 25 miles a week without undue stress; (3) you have competed in track meets or road races and have begun to experience diminishing returns; and (4) you now want to improve your performances by modifying your training. If one or more of these factors are missing, you may want to train using the program outlined at the end of chapter 1.

The following schedule provides for a long run once a week, increasing in distance from 6 to 16 miles. (The weekly mileage also gradually builds from 20 to 40 miles.) A midweek "semi-long" run increases from 4 to 9 miles. Another day features some easy speedwork to offer a slight change of pace and to hint at the interval training that will come during a later phase of your training. But don't push too hard on this "speed" day; there will be time for faster training later.

Also avoid running the "easy" days too hard, and don't skip the rest days. These are particularly essential for balancing the weekly long runs that are the key to building endurance.

Depending on your level of ability, you may want to begin with a slightly higher weekly mileage by increasing the length of your longer runs. But don't feel that you *must* increase your longest run. Sixteen miles, or 2 hours of running, is an ample distance goal for even fast athletes.

The best time to build an aerobic base is after the end of a long competitive season. Ease back on your training for one or two weeks and begin as follows.

**Weeks 1 and 2 (20 miles each week)**
**Sunday:** 6-mile run, steady
**Monday:** rest
**Tuesday:** 4 miles, jogging and walking
**Wednesday:** 2-mile jog
**Thursday:** 4-mile run, steady
**Friday:** 2-mile jog
**Saturday:** 2-mile jog

**Weeks 3 and 4 (24 miles each week)**
**Sunday:** 8-mile run, steady
**Monday:** rest
**Tuesday:** 4 miles, jogging and walking
**Wednesday:** 2-mile jog
**Thursday:** 5-mile run, steady
**Friday:** 3-mile jog
**Saturday:** 2-mile jog

**Weeks 5 and 6 (28 miles each week)**
**Sunday:** 10-mile run, steady
**Monday:** rest
**Tuesday:** 4-mile run, running and jogging
**Wednesday:** 2-mile jog

*(continued)*

## BUILDING AN AEROBIC BASE—*Continued*

**Thursday:** 6-mile run, steady
**Friday:** 4-mile jog
**Saturday:** 2-mile jog

### Weeks 7 and 8 (32 miles each week)

**Sunday:** 12-mile run, steady
**Monday:** rest
**Tuesday:** 4-mile run, running and jogging
**Wednesday:** 2-mile jog
**Thursday:** 7-mile run, steady
**Friday:** 4-mile jog
**Saturday:** 3-mile jog

### Weeks 9 and 10 (36 miles each week)

**Sunday:** 14-mile run, steady
**Monday:** rest
**Tuesday:** 4 miles, including easy sprints
**Wednesday:** 2-mile jog
**Thursday:** 8-mile run, steady
**Friday:** 5-mile jog
**Saturday:** 3-mile jog

### Weeks 11 and 12 (40 miles each week)

**Sunday:** 16-mile run, steady
**Monday:** rest
**Tuesday:** 4 miles, including easy sprints
**Wednesday:** 3-mile jog
**Thursday:** 9-mile run, steady
**Friday:** 5-mile jog
**Saturday:** 3-mile jog

You will be able to move into the speed phase of your training after this 12-week program—assuming that you are able to complete it without excess stress or becoming injured. At the end of this base training period, you might want to run a race at one of your competitive distances to test your level of conditioning. That will also help you establish a pace for your later speedwork.

Smith's Olympic performance; in actuality, it was one of the reasons she ran so well in Seoul.

Larrieu Smith's long runs maintained her aerobic base and, in effect, kept her oxygen delivery system open. With this sound base remaining in place, she was better able to benefit from the anaerobic (speed) training she also was doing.

Other women who were coached by Vaughan trained only anaerobically and found that without as sound an aerobic base, they could not maintain their peak conditioning that long into the season.

# Chapter 3

# SPEED ENDURANCE

## WHERE TIME AND INTENSITY MEET

**R**ussell H. Pate, Ph.D., director of the Human Performance Laboratory at the University of South Carolina and a former 2:15:00 marathoner, believes that even well-trained runners can improve speed by simply improving endurance. He links the two concepts in a single term: *speed endurance.*

Dr. Pate defines endurance as the ability to continue activity of a designated intensity for a prolonged period. You go far. But speed endurance couples the ability to go far with the ability to go fast. In other words, you attain the ability to go farther faster.

"In 10-K terminology," says Dr. Pate, "you're talking about an ability to maintain intensities ranging from 85 to 95 percent of your $VO_2$ max for a period of a half hour or longer."

# *MEET VO$_2$ MAX*

Before moving on, let's define *VO$_2$ max*. This term is often used by researchers as a convenient benchmark to measure human performance, but runners frequently confuse it with another "max" more often used by doctors and coaches: maximum heart rate, or MHR.

Your VO$_2$ max relates to the maximum volume of oxygen transported to your muscles. In other words, it represents your body's aerobic power potential, your ability to deliver oxygen to those muscles, particularly for endurance activity. Usually scientists obtain the measurement by monitoring athletes who are running on a treadmill or riding an exercise bike while breathing into a device that measures gas volume. This permits researchers to arrive at a figure that defines the amount of oxygen an athlete can consume per kilogram of body weight per minute (ml/kg/min).

That's the researchers' max. Then there's the doctors' max: MHR. Sports physicians and/or coaches find it the best measure of ability, since they are dedicated to training athletes rather than testing them. MHR is just what it says. It's the maximum number of times your heart beats under extreme stress, usually measured in terms of 1 minute. (A well-trained athlete might have an MHR near 220, depending on age and level of training.)

With the exception of this chapter, you'll encounter the term MHR more frequently than VO$_2$ max in this book, because I believe MHR is easier to measure and put to use. You can measure your MHR with some accuracy using only a watch, but to measure your VO$_2$ max, you need to be tested at a human performance laboratory, which can be expensive and impossible for most people.

One hundred percent of VO$_2$ max is the same as 100 percent maximum heart rate, but after that, the two maxes diverge. For instance, to achieve 50 percent of VO$_2$ max, you actually exercise at 75 percent of your MHR. It's also possible to achieve levels above 100 percent of VO$_2$ max, at least for short periods of time. In dealing with MHR, 100 percent is the max. In most cases, it serves our purpose best to stick with the latter measurement: the doctors' max, or MHR.

# THE MECHANICS OF SPEED ENDURANCE

Dr. Pate believes that three major physiological factors contribute to speed endurance.

**Oxygen uptake:** This refers to the maximum volume of oxygen your body can transport and absorb. It's the origin of the term $VO_2$ *max.*

**Lactate threshhold:** Some individuals start to accumulate lactic acid sooner than others. "An untrained person may accumulate lactic acid at as low as 30 to 40 percent of their $VO_2$ max," says Dr. Pate. Their lactate threshold is very low. "More highly trained endurance athletes, on the other hand, will be able to work at 80 percent or more without accumulating lactic acid." They have developed a high lactate threshold, so they can perform longer and harder at sub-max levels. Dr. Pate notes that $VO_2$ max sets a cap on the entire system. "I don't think we've ever found an individual who can work more than a few minutes at 100 percent of $VO_2$ max," he says, "because you start accumulating lactic acid too rapidly."

**Efficiency:** This relates to biomechanics and economy of motion. The smoother the runner, the less oxygen he or she consumes at a particular running speed. "The lower the rate of oxygen consumption, the lower the amount of metabolic and cardiorespiratory stress, and the farther you can run," says Dr. Pate. Efficiency, scientists agree, is most difficult to modify by training. (In chapter 5, I'll discuss efficient running form in detail.)

"To acquire endurance, you need to put these three factors together," Dr. Pate explains. "The optimum would be to have a high $VO_2$ max, have a high lactate threshold, and be very economical." A program that develops these three factors produces high-powered performances.

# *ACQUIRING*
# *SPEED ENDURANCE*

Some of your endurance capacity is natural. If you possess an ability to endure, it is probably because you have a higher percentage of slow-twitch than fast-twitch muscles. Thus, genes determine our endurance capacity. To improve base endurance, we train. "Anybody, regardless of their muscle composition, can improve endurance with training," says Ball State researcher Dr. David Costill.

But to develop speed endurance, you need to use specific types of training. How do you achieve that end? Let's begin by expanding our discussion from chapter 2 on developing your base endurance.

Improving endurance requires muscle adaptations, claims William Fink, who works closely with Dr. Costill at the Human Performance Laboratory at Ball State. The key, says Fink, is producing more mitochondria, a subcellular organelle that makes adenosine triphosphate (ATP), the energy that fuels your muscles. "When someone exercises aerobically," Fink explains, "we see increased activity in a number of specific enzymes involved in the utilization of ATP. The muscle also develops more capillaries, which enhance the delivery of blood and oxygen to the muscle."

According to Stan James, M.D., an orthopedic surgeon from Eugene, Oregon, who runs and cross-country skis: "There's a certain amount of endurance associated with increased strength, which also comes with endurance training." Dr. Pate adds: "The muscle develops more connective tissue, a larger cross section. All of this improves endurance."

The key to endurance training, according to Dr. Pate, is to gradually increase your exercise stress. He explains: "In order to induce an adaptation, you have to force the system to do something it is not currently adapted to. The trick is to apply a stress sufficient to adapt the system without the undesirable side effects and injuries that come with doing too much. This all needs to be *individualized*. People vary in how much exercise they can tolerate."

Nevertheless, scientists can now state with some precision how much training is necessary for the average runner to improve his endurance, specifically his *speed* endurance. Howard A. Wenger and Gordon J. Bell of the School of Education of the University of Victoria in British Columbia have identified three factors necessary to achieve maximal gains in aerobic power, the essential quality of speed endurance. They are intensity, frequency, and duration.

### INTENSITY

According to Wenger and Bell: "The magnitude of change in $VO_2$ max increases as exercise intensity increases from 50 to 100 percent $VO_2$ max, and then begins to fall as the intensity exceeds $VO_2$ max."

That statement certainly requires some explanation because of possible confusion, again between the scientists' max and the doctors' max. To begin to get improvement in your $VO_2$ max, you must exercise at an intensity equal to at least 50 percent of your $VO_2$ max. This means you need to train at 75 percent of your MHR, a pace that we might call your minimum aerobic pace. (The better condition you are in, the harder you have to train to improve your $VO_2$ max. For higher-intensity workouts, see "Pace 1" on the opposite page.)

*Translation:* To improve endurance, train at 75 percent of your MHR or higher.

### FREQUENCY

Wenger and Bell further state: "Improvements in $VO_2$ max are greater in both absolute and relative terms up to six sessions per week (for low fitness). In the high-fitness category, however, no improvements are elicited with only two sessions per week, and maximal gains accrue at a frequency of four."

*Translation:* To improve endurance, train at race pace four times a week, approximately every other day.

### DURATION

Wenger and Bell note some improvements in training sessions of 15 to 30 minutes. They identify the most improvements when exercise exceeds 35 minutes. They write: "This improvement could reflect the greater involvement of fast-twitch motor units as slow-twitch units begin to fatigue."

Beyond 45 minutes, however, improvements decline, most likely because it becomes difficult to maintain intensity (as described previously) for that long a time or to train that hard with the right frequency.

*Translation:* To improve endurance, the hard portion of your average workout should last 35 to 45 minutes.

To summarize the results of the Wenger and Bell survey: The combination of intensity and frequency that elicits the greatest absolute and relative change is 75 to 90 percent of MHR four times per week, with exercise durations of 35 to 45 minutes. The scientists add: "It is important to note that lower intensities still produce effective changes and reduce the risks of injury in nonathletic groups."

# SMART TRAINING

One of the appeals of an endurance sport is that you can overcome a lack of natural ability—considered by many the most essential ingredient for success—with dedication and training. Acquiring speed endurance requires some natural talent, of course, but with the mental focus to train hard—and to train *smart*—anyone can develop a faster, stronger pace.

Dr. Pate, drawing on both his research as an exercise physiologist and his own experiences as a world-class marathoner, believes that smart training is the key to improving speed endurance. What is smart training? One key factor, he claims, is regular pace changes.

## PACE 1 (HIGH INTENSITY)

"For decades," says Dr. Pate, "exercise physiologists have studied changes in $VO_2$ max, and it's modifiable. I think it's debatable whether or not we know the best way to modify $VO_2$ max, but clearly, high-intensity activity is a key.

*(continued on page 30)*

# PLOT YOUR
# SPEED ENDURANCE PROGRAM

The training programs used by many top runners are similar to those suggested by Howard Wenger and Gordon Bell of the University of Victoria in British Columbia, Dr. Russell Pate of the University of South Carolina, and others quoted in this book. They offer a blend of hard work and easy work, fast running and slow running, all combined with adequate rest.

Keeping in mind the principles covered in this chapter, here is one way of structuring a program to develop speed endurance. (Paces 1, 2, 3, and 4 relate to the various intensities described in "Smart Training" on page 27.)

### Sunday: Long Run
**Distance:** 10 to 20 miles
**Time:** 90 to 180 minutes
**Intensity:** low
**Pace 3:** 1 to 2 minutes slower than race pace
**Purpose:** to strengthen aerobic base

### Monday: Rest
**Distance:** 3 to 6 miles
**Time:** 20 to 40 minutes
**Intensity:** low
**Pace 3:** 1 to 2 minutes slower than race pace
**Purpose:** to recuperate from yesterday's long run

### Tuesday: Speedwork
**Distance:** 3 to 6 miles
**Time:** 20 to 40 minutes (repetition training)

**Intensity:** high
**Pace 1:** race pace
**Purpose:** to increase $VO_2$ max and efficiency

*Wednesday: Rest*
**Distance:** 3 to 6 miles
**Time:** 20 to 40 minutes
**Intensity:** low
**Pace 3:** 1 to 2 minutes slower than race pace
**Purpose:** to recuperate from yesterday's speedwork

*Thursday: Lactate Threshold Run*
**Distance:** 5 to 10 miles
**Time:** 30 to 60 minutes
**Intensity:** medium
**Pace 2:** 15 to 30 seconds slower than race pace
**Purpose:** to increase lactate threshold

*Friday: Rest*
**Distance:** 0 to 6 miles
**Time:** 0 to 40 minutes
**Intensity:** low
**Pace 3 or 4:** 1 to 2 minutes slower than race pace
**Purpose:** to recuperate for weekend of hard work

*Saturday: Swing Day*
**Distance:** 5 to 10 miles
**Time:** 30 to 60 minutes
**Intensity:** medium to high
**Pace 1 or 2:** race pace or slightly slower
**Purpose:** competition, or other fast training

Exercising at intensities that go beyond the individual's current $VO_2$ max is important."

What type of training would this be? A typical Pace 1 workout would be three 1-mile repeats, with 5 minutes or more of walking or jogging in between. (A *repeat* is any distance run at a set pace, followed by fairly complete rest and repeated runs at that distance.) Dr. Pate suggests a speed faster than the pace of your last 10-K. A runner capable of a 37-minute 10-K, for instance, would run his repeats at a 6-minute-mile pace or faster. (For more on repeats, see chapter 7.)

One side benefit of working out at race pace is that it gets you to recruit fast-twitch muscle fibers, according to Dr. Pate. "If those fibers have not been used in training, they may not be recruited easily when we get into a competitive situation."

## PACE 2 (MEDIUM INTENSITY)

Also important to training are lactate threshold runs. (The lactate threshold in a trained runner would be 80 to 90 percent of his $VO_2$ max.)

Dr. Pate prescribes running longer but somewhat slower in Pace 2 workouts, about 20 to 60 minutes at 70 to 90 percent of your MHR. "Not as fast as an interval workout, but faster than the pace used on a long run," he instructs. In other words, set a pace slower than your 10-K time. The runner capable of a 6-minute-mile pace, for example, would do lactate threshold runs at about a 6:20 pace.

When Dr. Pate was training for the Boston Marathon (he placed second there in 1975 and 1977), he would add a lactate threshold run to his Saturday routine as a prelude to his Sunday long runs.

He picked that workout intuitively. Later, as an exercise physiologist, he understood its scientific base. "Recent training studies have looked specifically at how to increase endurance performance," he says, "and some evidence suggests prolonged activity at intensities close to your current lactate threshold is helpful to increase that threshold."

## PACE 3 (LOW INTENSITY)

This is the longer run taken at a slower pace—everybody's typical Sunday morning workout. Many runners who are training for a marathon, for instance, choose 20 miles as the distance for their long run. They run aerobically, at a steady pace near 70 percent of their MHR. "Longer runs are valuable," says Dr. Pate, "even if you're not training for a marathon."

The pace used in low-intensity runs should be slow enough so that you can converse with your training partners. A runner capable of a 6-minute-mile pace in a 10-K would run at a 7- to 8-minute-mile pace (or slower) on long runs. Someone less speedy would run slower still.

## PACE 4 (REST)

Equally important is rest, which might consist of slow running at short distances or a day off. "Some people do quite a lot of running on their recovery days," according to Dr. Pate, "but for others, any activity should be minimal. If they do too much on rest days, they either are going to get injured or they become so tired they need to back off on their hard days, which defeats the purpose of the entire training plan."

Dr. Pate considers variety the key to any training program. He also subscribes to periodization, or peaking. "I continue to be attracted to the concept of building on intensity as one works toward achieving a major goal in some particular competition," he says. "There is risk associated with high-intensity exercise. Experience indicates that such workouts are more demanding and stressful. Carrying on high-frequency training for prolonged periods is risky in terms of overtraining and even riskier in terms of injury."

So to improve your speed endurance, surround your key sessions with sound recovery activities—like easy, short runs, swimming, or walking. Build your program on priorities. The highest priority is attached to the key hard sessions, so take the rest days necessary to prevent breakdown and injury.

# Chapter 4

# PERFOR-MANCE BOOSTERS

## THE BEST WARM-UPS FOR SMOOTH RUNNING

**M**any runners fail to recognize the value of a thorough warm-up. While competing in the Fall Frolic Four, a 4-mile race in Hammond, Indiana, I noticed that only a few of the participants took the time to warm up; probably a minority of that minority warmed up well. Sure, a number of runners popped out of the gym 15 or 20 minutes before the start of that cold and windy day to briefly jog up and down the street, but I suspect that was the extent of the warm-up for most.

Warming up is rarely discussed. And it's complicated by the fact that runners fanning the fitness boom today never participated in track in high school, where they might have been coached in the values of warm-up. Everybody knows about stretching, but that's only part of a good warm-up.

How important is a good warm-up? It probably won't lower your race time by more than a few seconds—well, let's say 5 to 10 seconds. That seems inconsequential over the length of a 10-K race that lasts more than a half hour—unless you are shoulder to shoulder with some friend you've wanted to beat for four years. But let's face facts: You wouldn't be reading this book if you didn't want to shave every possible second off your performance. At the elite level, hundredths of a second can make a difference of thousands of dollars.

A good warm-up routine is also valuable for preventing injuries. Cold muscles are more likely to pull than warm muscles. Then there is the matter of comfort. You can run more relaxed when warm than when cold. Minor irritations such as side stitches are less likely to occur if you warm up before going to the line. And since psychological considerations often overshadow physical talents when it comes to success, a good warm-up can focus your mind as much as your body. By warming up thoroughly, you signal your body that this is a day for running fast.

Of course, warming up is an inconvenience, a bother. You have to get to the start earlier than you might otherwise. At many races, getting an adequate warm-up is difficult, if not outright impossible. At major races with several thousand entrants, you may be forced to go to the line early and wait to hold your spot on the starting grid. This can be quite a handicap, particularly for a short race. In a marathon, you often can start slow, planning to warm up gradually over the first few miles. But you can't afford to start too slowly in races of only a few miles. It's a simple fact of racing life: The shorter the race, the faster the pace, the warmer your muscles need to be to reach full speed rapidly.

Certainly, warm-up is most important in race situations, because you go from a standing start to full speed within seconds after hearing the starter's gun. But a good warm-up with stretching should not be overlooked during training either, particularly on those hard days when you run fast repetitions on the track.

Warm-up is particularly important for running in cold

weather, when the temperature falls below 50°F and runners don extra clothes to retain body heat. On the other hand, don't assume that you can skip the warm-up during warm weather because you are hot and sweaty. Pay special attention to warm-up on those days when you feel you need it the least. Your muscles will still need the extra performance boost that warm-ups deliver.

All told, warm-up is a subject to which every runner should give full consideration. So let's do just that, beginning with warm-up before workouts and later considering warm-up before races.

# THE WARM-UP
# BEFORE THE WORKOUT

Few runners have time to spend an hour warming up before their daily workouts. Nevertheless, as I've already said, the faster you plan to run, the more you need to warm up. Here's how to do it right.

## MAKE IT A HABIT

In working with high school runners, I try to instill good warm-up habits, which is not easy to do. One problem is that every runner needs to find a warm-up routine to suit his or her rhythms. But team unity prohibits having two dozen runners warming up two dozen ways, particularly in cross-country, where the team usually tours the course as part of their warm-up. In track, runners more often can warm up on their own, since they compete in different events.

At the beginning of the season, I set aside one workout where we practice warming up and nothing else. We go through it by the numbers. We even use the routine as a complete workout the day before a meet. We simply jog, stretch, stride, and jog, then go home.

Obtaining a proper warm-up often can be a problem at midweek races and meets held away from our home track. Once we arrive after an hour-long bus ride, we have barely 30 minutes to get ready to run. So you do the best you can.

Most runners in open races don't have this problem, since they're not required to arrive or leave with a team. So they have no excuse for not warming up properly.

Can proper warm-up help you avoid injury? Can it make you a faster runner? I believe the answer to both questions is yes. Warm-up and cool-down should limit the damage you can do to your body, particularly when used before and after the intense workouts that are the heart of any program designed to help you run fast.

There are three components to my workout warm-up, which I also stress to my high school runners. These steps are simple, and they prepare my muscles for a productive workout. One, I jog for 10 to 20 minutes. Two, I go through my stretching routine, as I describe below. And three, my final step, I do a set of three or four easy sprints of 50 to 150 meters. These serve to "awaken" my muscles.

## A DOZEN WAYS TO STRETCH FOR SUCCESS

Stretching is a subject that has launched a thousand magazine illustrations, but most runners probably can figure out how to stretch on their own or by watching other runners. If you want to learn from a book, I'd recommend Bob Anderson's *Stretching*.

Also check out the American Running and Fitness Association's (ARFA) four-page pamphlet on stretching. It illustrates stretches that implement the following ARFA recommendations: Never stretch a cold muscle; use the static stretch; don't bounce or lunge; breathe relaxed and naturally; never stretch to the point of pain; ease into and out of the stretch slowly and rhythmically; and concentrate on how you feel in the stretch. To order the pamphlet, contact ARFA at 9310 Old Georgetown Road, Bethesda, MD 20814; (301) 897–0197.

I developed my own standard stretching routine over a period of time, without any particular scientific basis other than it feels good to me. I suggest you do the same. The purpose of stretching preworkout, prerace, or pre-anything is to make you feel good as well as to get loose. Don't do some exercise just because you saw it in Anderson's book or because every other runner you know stretches that way. If it doesn't work for you, don't do it. Anderson would tell you the same.

Having said that, let me tell you that most of my stretches flow from one to another. That wastes less time, which is important if you have a limited period for a stretching routine. Here's the Higdon list of stretches.

**Overhead reach:** Stand with your feet slightly spread and reach overhead. Focus on your posture and reach for the sky. Personally, I enjoy another version of this stretch. When I run to the nearby golf course, there's a favorite evergreen tree with a branch just in my reach. I hang from it and enjoy the aromatic smell of the tree. But you can stand anywhere that you find a cubic meter of ground and do this stretch. It's my opener.

**Hang ten:** Stand with your feet slightly spread, bend forward from the waist, and let your fingers dangle toward the ground. The farther your legs are spread, the easier it is to touch the ground. But there is no shame in this. If some other runner tells me my knees are slightly bent, I ask them how fast they ran their last 10-K. Unless it was 5 minutes faster than I've run, I don't listen to their advice. Again, do what works best for you.

**Twist and turn:** Still standing, put your hands on your hips, bend at the waist, and rotate slowly—forward, sideways, and back. Do a few rotations in the clockwise direction, then in the counterclockwise direction. Wait a minute, you say, isn't stretching supposed to be static? I'll check my rule book and leave a message on your telephone answering machine.

**Heel holds:** Support yourself with one hand on a wall or tree, and grasp your ankle with the other hand, pulling it toward your buttocks. There are two ways to do heel holds. One way is to grasp your left ankle with the right hand, then your right ankle with your left hand. The other way is to grasp your left ankle with your left hand, then your right ankle with your right hand. Various experts have written why one heel hold is superior to the other. I some-times do one, sometimes the other, sometimes both, sometimes neither. I don't want to offend the experts by playing favorites.

**Wall lean:** Every runner knows this one. It's a safe, effective way to stretch your calf muscles. Find a wall, or a stationary object such as a tree, and stand about 2 feet away from it. Keep your heels planted firmly on the ground, and place your hands on the wall, shoulder width apart. Keeping your back straight, bend your elbows and gently lean forward. It feels good, plus it's an excellent stretch before fast races, where the calf muscles come into play.

There are a couple of variations on the wall lean. One is to lean with both feet together; another is to lean with one foot forward (knee bent) and one foot back, then switch. Take your pick. A massage therapist I visited in Duluth, Minnesota, following Grandma's Marathon taught me an interesting variation of the split-leg wall lean. After stretching in one position, you move the front foot left and/or right, which stretches slightly different muscle combinations.

To stretch your calf muscles without the wall, stand tiptoe on stairs, allowing your heels to hang over the edge. Do the same going up escalators, too. Never miss an opportunity for a good stretch.

**The great behind:** Hit the deck now—literally. Squat to get low enough to touch the floor with your hands near your behind. Then simply roll over backward, gently, with your toes pointing upward, your knees tucked against your forehead, and your arms spread wide at a 45-degree angle for balance. This is the Higdon equivalent of contemplating your navel while everybody else at the race contemplates something else. But don't be self-conscious; your object is to get loose.

**Hurdle:** Sit on the floor with your legs in front of you. Bend your left leg to the side, and keep your right leg straight in front of you. Support yourself with your left hand, and reach for your toes with your right. Only reach as far as comfortably possible, without any pain. Don't force this stretch. After you've stretched your right leg, switch your position to stretch your left.

To do this stretch effectively, try to picture what Edwin

Moses looks like going over the 400-meter hurdles. I have a signed poster from him on my basement wall, and his front leg is bent. If Edwin Moses can run a world record 47.13 with a bent leg, I see no reason why lesser runners should force their legs flat against the floor in this stretch.

**Butterfly:** While you're sitting on the floor, again put your legs straight in front of you. Bend your knees so that they're pointing out to the sides and your feet are touching sole to sole. In this position, wrap your hands around your feet and press outward with your arms against the inside of your thighs, extending the stretch.

**Knee pull:** Lie flat on your back, and with your knee bent, bring one leg toward your chest, assisting it by pulling with both hands just below the knee. Do the same with your other leg. I've been doing this stretch for years for no other reason than it feels good, but I saw the stretch pictured in a *Runner's World* article titled "An Ounce of Prevention." I must be on the right track.

**Horizontal reach:** This is just like the overhead reach, the first stretch in this list, except now you're lying on your back. Point your toes and reach above your head with your fingertips. Hold the stretch as long as it feels comfortable, then roll over and do the horizontal reach again, this time facedown. I pretend I'm 7 feet tall and playing in the National Basketball Association. This is a comfortable stretch that I feel I could hold forever, but I seldom maintain a stretch as long as the de rigueur 30 seconds recommended by other experts.

**Belt-down push-ups:** I use this push-up variation not to strengthen my arms but to loosen my back. The position is the same as for regular push-ups, except that your lower body remains "nailed" to the ground and you push up only the upper body. I usually do about five of these.

**Starter's crouch:** Few distance runners will find themselves in this position in a race situation, but I find it an effective stretching exercise. Pretending you're Carl Lewis at the start of the 100 meters, rise into a set position, but with the back leg fully extended. This gives you another variation on the wall lean. (But don't attempt to press your heel flat on the ground.) Switch legs, hold the stretch, then switch legs back and forth rapidly—a dynamic stretch. Remember, I don't limit myself to static stretches.

This ends the floor portion of my stretching routine. I rise and repeat one or two of the standing stretches with which I began my routine, most often the overhead reach or the twist and turn. If time is short, I may skip some stretches.

Can I complete a dozen stretches, some of them involving several variations, in 5 to 10 minutes? Sure. Each stretch flows from one to the other, and I hold each only as long as I feel comfortable. This way I don't waste time. I'm not out to set an endurance record for stretching; I'm out to stretch to get ready for a comfortable, productive run. I follow my workout with an easy jog to cool down. It helps prevent injuries and keeps me in top form for racing.

# A WARM-UP FOR THE FINAL HOUR

Let me tell you about my personal warm-up routine before each race. I like to arrive between 60 and 90 minutes before race time. Sometimes I'll cut it closer for a race I'm treating mostly as a hard workout (a summer fun run, for instance), but an hour is almost minimal for any race in which I hope to perform well. Arriving early allows me time to pick up my number and visit the washrooms before I start my warm-up countdown. One plus in getting there early: You won't have to waste as much time standing in lines.

On some occasions, I'll do a *pre*—warm-up at home before climbing into the car to go to the race. This pre—warm-up may be less than a mile, just enough to loosen my bowels so I can visit the toilet before leaving for the race. I may stop for gas en route if I need another pit stop. And in the last few minutes of my drive, I'm still scouting for hidden toilets without people standing in line. You can waste a good warm-up by being forced to stand in line for 10 to 15 minutes because the race organizers failed to provide adequate rest room facilities.

One advantage that road races have over track meets is

that you can predict with some certainty the time the race will begin. If the entry blank announces a start at 8:00 A.M., most well-organized races will begin precisely at that time. At track meets, the mere number of scheduled races often causes delays, or races start earlier than stated, which is sometimes worse. Track runners often need to be more adaptable about their warm-up than road runners.

## 60 MINUTES AND COUNTING

Sixty minutes before race time, I usually start my count-down. I try to use the same routine before each race, certainly before the important ones, because it is a routine that works for me. Here's how it goes.

**Jog (10 to 20 minutes):** How far I go in my prerace jog depends on how loose I feel arriving at the start. A drive of more than an hour to the race, or hard training the week before from which I haven't fully recovered, may require me to spend more time (and warm up more slowly). Generally, I like to go a couple of miles in my warm-up.

If I am familiar with the area, I may jog to a location where I do the remainder of my warm-up alone. It depends partly on how much the race means to me. Before important races, I may not want to waste my concentration chatting with other runners.

**Relax (5 to 10 minutes):** If I have not yet picked up my number, now is the time I do it. This may be time for another visit to the toilet, although everybody else has the same idea at this time.

**Stretch (5 to 10 minutes):** I try to find some quiet area (not always easy at large races) where I have enough room to stretch without being disturbed by too many people. If it's warm, I prefer to stretch outdoors on the grass, under the shade of a tree. As with my workout warm-up, I begin with standing stretches, move to floor stretches, and finish by repeating some of the standing stretches.

## T MINUS 30

With 30 minutes left, I usually have finished stretching. At this point, I move into the next phase of my warm-up.

**Flexible play (5 to 10 minutes):** This is a dynamic extension of my stretching routine that includes bounding and strides, with jogging and walking in between. I don't utilize my full set of bounding exercises (as I describe in chapter 6) but do at most two or three. High knees and high heels are handy because they are simple and less stressful. (See the sections on "High Knees" and "High Heels" on pages 67 and 69, respectively.) You might find them helpful, too. But try them out in your workout first. Don't include bounding in your race warm-up unless you bound regularly as part of your training.

More essential are the strides. Run three or four easy sprints of 50 to 150 meters at a pace not much faster than your race pace to remind your legs about the task at hand. I like to accelerate very gradually, hit a good pace in the middle, then gradually decelerate. I walk and jog between strides. Before a road race, I pick out a straight section of street for this routine. If possible, I choose a stretch that slants slightly downhill, doing my fast strides that way because it makes me feel faster. For the same reason, I always run my strides downwind.

In teaching warm-up to members of his team at Southwestern Michigan College, coach Ron Gunn has them do a 200-meter run at race pace exactly 20 minutes before race time. I've followed this approach on occasion and feel it works particularly well on those days when nothing you do seems to loosen you up. Just pushing that extra distance at a fast pace seems to do it. Yes, you'll use energy that you may otherwise have conserved for the race, but in 5-K and 10-K races, energy conservation is not usually a problem. You should have ample energy for the job at hand; if a long stride during the prerace warm-up aids your ability to get loose, do it.

Another variation on this routine is to do three strides of increasing length: 20, 30, and 40 seconds, or 100, 150, and 200 meters.

**Final preparations (10 to 15 minutes):** The warm-up has ended. What remains is to get ready to race. Usually I wait until now to don my racing top, preferring to go to the line with a dry shirt rather than one wet with sweat. On a cool day, I want to avoid getting even slightly chilled and losing the benefits of the warm-up. Also, I warm up in training shoes, then change to my lighter race models.

I carefully knot my shoelaces to prevent them from coming untied midway through a race. This happened to me only once, while racing in the Vulcan Run, a 10-K in Birmingham, Alabama. It was maybe 2 miles into the race, and I didn't want to run the rest of the way with shoelaces dangling, so I stopped to tie them. I figure it cost me at least 30 seconds. To avoid a recurrence, I tie my shoes once, then jog to the line. By the time I reach the line, the laces have loosened somewhat, so I pull them snugger and tie them again with a double knot. Finally, I tie a square knot over that. Removing my shoes takes time after the race, but I accept that.

In the last few minutes, I do some easy jogging and maybe take one or two more very short strides or stretch some more. Waiting for the gun, I let my arms hang and shake my wrists in a last-minute battle with my nerves.

At high school races, the starter often tells the runners to "shag out," meaning they sprint off the line for 50 to 75 meters, then gather in a circle to give a team cheer before jogging back to the start. The physiological reason for the shag is to elevate the pulse rate to a point where the heart can pump blood with immediate efficiency. In my case (and this probably is also true of most well-trained runners), my pulse rate returns to normal so rapidly that I would need to make such a sprint within the final minute to guarantee a high pulse rate at the start. But the dynamics of most road races rarely permit shag-outs by large numbers of runners. So I suggest you simply wait patiently, with the knowledge that, having followed the warm-up routine in this chapter, you are as hot to trot as anyone else in the field. The gun sounds. And you're off!

## WHEN ALL IS SAID AND DONE

Almost as fast as it starts, the race is over. You've crossed the finish line, and hopefully, your PR has taken a move for the better. You're ready to go home now, right? Wrong. There's one more thing left to do—your cool-down.

A cool-down obviously won't aid you in running the race you just completed any faster, but it will help you recuperate more rapidly. It also helps you return to regular training more quickly, resulting in a stronger performance the next time you race.

Within 5 minutes after crossing the finish line, I begin my cool-down at the same pace as, but for half the distance of, my warm-up jog. On cool days, I don sweats. On warm days, I won't wait to change. As long as it doesn't interfere with the other runners, I like to turn around and jog back over the course, since it gives me an opportunity to see my friends finish. Sometimes I turn around and meet them at the line so we can cool down together. This is the beginning of the social hour.

Scientists may tell you that you should cool down to help process the removal of lactic acid and other waste products that may have pooled in your muscles during your final anaerobic sprint. This, they say, will prevent muscle soreness. That's only partially true. Lactic acid largely disappears from your system within a half hour, whether or not you do a cool-down. The soreness and stiffness experienced after a race is more from minute muscle fiber tears than from lactic acid.

Cool-down is also a fun way to cap the experience. It gives you time to think about your race alone, and time to share it with others, if you like.

And the better shape you are in, the more you will enjoy this social time. In fact, that's one benefit of running short races. I've never been able to do much immediately after a marathon, other than stare at the cup of yogurt in my hand and wonder how I'm going to summon enough energy to walk back to my hotel clad in a silly aluminum blanket. But 5 minutes after most shorter races, I'm ready to run again.

# Chapter 5

# FORM ENHANCERS

## WIPE OUT FLAWS TO INCREASE SPEED

**T**o witness running at its basic level, attend an elementary school track meet. Not an age-group race where children often have the benefit of coaching, good or bad, but a school meet where kids have been pulled off the playground and told to go run. You see the human body in motion before coaching, before training. This is not necessarily running at its prettiest, merely at its purest.

One spring afternoon, my wife, Rose, a sixth-grade teacher, suggested I attend an elementary school track meet where some of her students were running. She's not a coach, but she thought it would be nice if I would offer some encouragement to the runners. "Just stop by and say hello," she said. So I did.

A girl named Lisa caught my eye. One of the slenderest in the field, she was running in the fifth-grade 400-meter run, the longest event for girls her age. Lisa started slowly, and she was near last through the first turn. But as the field rushed down the back straightaway, several early sprinters faltered. Lisa passed them, moving at a steady pace. Into the turn, she caught several more. On the final straightaway, she was catching the leader, a girl who was bigger, stronger, and probably older. Lisa finished a smooth second. Her easy, natural form and consistent pace were the key to her impressive finish. And this wasn't her first good show. She also finished second in the 50-meter dash earlier in the meet.

(When Lisa reached high school age, I knew I wanted her on my cross-country team. Knowing she would be running, I already had an advance scouting report on her. She was the younger sister of the top runner on my boys' team, Tony Morales. Perhaps she had some genetic advantages that predisposed her to being a good runner. It seemed to me that Lisa was a natural.)

The meet then moved on to the sixth-grade 600-meter run, the distance event for that class. This time I wasn't really watching for any particular runner, so I sat back to enjoy the race. A half dozen runners burst ahead at the start, but one girl caught my attention. She showed superior running form. She was smooth and efficient. At the end, she caught all but one.

Later, I learned her name was Courtney. Both Lisa and Courtney soon would reach high school age. Visions of state championships danced in my head. Of course, events could interfere. They might mature into something other than skinny runners, or they might choose a sport like golf or volleyball. They might find other interests. But at that stage in their life, Lisa and Courtney shared one talent that would have caused any track coach to pick them out of a crowd: economy.

# RUNNERS' ECONOMICS

It is a skill that's sometimes overlooked when experts discuss what makes a good distance runner. We know we need strong legs, a strong heart, and a strong mind to run fast, and it also helps to have only about 10 percent body fat. But one important factor that determines whether you finish near the front or rear of your local 10-K race is an efficient running style, or effective biomechanics. Most runners call it good form.

We can try to change our form, but only to a certain point. A good coach can tell a runner how to incline his head, how to hold his arms, how to land on his feet, how to look like a refined runner. "We spend a lot of time on body awareness," says Sam Bell, Indiana University track coach. But coaching can only refine what Mother Nature gave you. Some of us are born with an efficient form, and some of us have to take the form we have and learn to *make* it efficient. But even a "natural" can profit from some guidance.

Ball State's Dr. David Costill remembers the time when three girls from one family, the Cartrights, began running road races in Muncie, Indiana. "When they started," recalls Dr. Costill, "they finished behind me, but as they got older, they gradually came up and finished in front of me." At age 13, Lora Cartwright, the oldest, set an age-group record of 2:55:00 in the marathon. She won several state championships and later competed for Purdue.

Dr. Costill continues: "The most noticeable thing from year to year was that they began as bouncers, because that's the way kids run. The older they got and the more they ran, the smoother they got. Jack Daniels did some research where he followed elementary and junior high school kids at six-month intervals, measuring their oxygen uptake while they ran at a set speed. What he learned was that as they got older, their $VO_2$ max didn't change. What happened was that they became more efficient. As a result, their times got faster. These improvements seem to be natural in young, developing kids, so the big question is: How do you improve the way more mature runners use their form?"

Dr. Costill believes that motor patterns developed early in life become "frozen." While subtle adjustments can be made in those motor patterns to improve performance, major changes will not occur. He cites speech patterns as an analogy, because they, too, become locked in place early. I have four cousins, for example, who emigrated from Italy to the United States at various ages, from 6 to 26. Each has an accent related to the age at which he or she arrived. If blindfolded, I would be able to identify their respective ages simply by the way they talk. Speech therapy and study can help them improve their speech patterns, but some accents still will remain.

Similarly, most coaches believe they can improve a runner's use of his form. Within a certain limit, they are correct. You may be able to make a silk purse out of a sow's ear, but you probably won't be able to convert that same ear into a new Camaro with a tape deck playing Dolly Parton's ten top hits. Scientists will tell you that economy is as much a genetic trait as slow-twitch fibers. We come from the womb preprogrammed for success or failure as runners, the biomechanical relationship of arms to legs to trunk already determined. There's no denying, for example, that no combination of dieting and training will ever convert William "The Refrigerator" Perry into an effective 10-K runner. Conversely, Pat Porter might be able to win eight consecutive TAC cross-country championships, but no amount of weight training will prepare him to play Perry's position of defensive tackle for the Chicago Bears.

Wherever an efficient running form comes from, a family tree or a coach's drill, Lisa and Courtney certainly have it. They were economical runners before any coach had a chance to work with them. As these girls grow older, time will tell whether they emerge as top runners.

As I learned from exercise physiologists and running coaches, an economical form is not achieved easily. Some experts even insist that it happens naturally, that it either cannot or should not be taught. Emil Zatopek had terrible upper-body form, yet he was possibly the greatest runner of all time. Alberto Salazar ran with the grace of a mailbag thrown from a truck, yet he set a world marathon record. "People run as they do because they have to," one college coach told me. "They don't have any choice. A lot of time is spent coaching things you don't have to, and this is one of them."

Yet coach Bell took exception to that statement when I repeated it to him. "What he's saying is that you can't coach. I happen to disagree with that."

Regardless of which point of view is correct, questions arise: Can your natural style or form be changed? How can you learn to run economically?

## POSITIVE GAINS

You *can* make your style more economical, even if you started running as an adult. Joanne Kittel is a perfect example. When she joined the beginning running class I taught, she was not the world's *least* economical runner, but she was close.

At one time, Kittel weighed 196 pounds. Over a period of years, before joining my class, she lost 80 of those pounds. So she at least *looked* like a runner—that is, when she was standing still. In motion, she was what Zorba the Greek might have called "the full catastrophe." She ran bent over, almost stumbling, gasping for breath. I was afraid to correct her running form for fear that any distraction would send her tumbling to the ground.

Kittel, however, persevered. She became every coach's dream—a runner with the desire to improve. Gradually, she built her running base. She went from an ability to jog 1 or 2 miles to an ability to cover 3 or 4 miles without tripping over a crack in the pavement. At classes and clinics, she paid attention when much swifter runners talked about speedwork. Soon Kittel was doing strides on the same golf course where I trained in the mornings. Later she did some interval training by making ¼-mile marks on a flat stretch of road that paralleled some railroad tracks. I taught her a few of these tricks, but mostly she learned by listening to others.

One morning, I was working in my study that overlooks Lake Shore Drive, a superhighway for joggers, walkers, and cyclists, particularly on Saturdays. I glanced out the window and saw this fast female striding smoothly past my house. It was Joanne Kittel! I remembered the stumbling woman who had seemed so uncoordinated when I first saw her in my class, and I was amazed. Kittel eventually would run 3:45:00 for the marathon, nowhere near the Olympic standard but a solid performance that many runners would be proud to emulate. Her achievements taught me that running economy can be a learnable trait, not merely a gift of genetics.

## LESS IS MORE

But exactly what *is* an economical runner? Owen Anderson, Ph.D., discussed the subject of economy in an article in *Running Research News:* "An economical runner is one who burns modest amounts of oxygen at a given pace; an uneconomical runner requires large amounts of oxygen (and energy) for the same running speed." In other words, when you're running at the same speed as your competitors, the pace feels easier to you than it does to them. Or when you're running with the same effort as your competitors, you're running faster than they are.

Dr. Anderson believes, as I do, that running economy is a neglected aspect of training. He indicated that while scientists seemingly have solved the secrets of boosting $VO_2$ max to create faster runners, little is known about which training methods best improve equally critical running economy, the skill that often separates good runners from bad.

In an article on running form that appeared in *The Runner,* I quoted a letter I received from Martyn Shorten, a professor from Loughborough University in Great Britain. "At any given constant running speed," Shorten wrote, "some runners consume less oxygen than others and may therefore be said to be more 'economic' in their use of oxygen. If two runners have the same maximum aerobic capacity, then the more 'economic' runner is likely to be capable of better performances." Shorten noted that this has been proved true both in the lab and on the track. "The better performers," he said, "are characterized by a combination of high $VO_2$ max and high running economy."

In spotting Lisa and Courtney in the grade school meet, I had instinctively recognized them as economical runners. They possessed one of the prerequisites necessary for success: They looked good while running. Because of their economy, they outperformed other untrained runners—at least at an early age. Without marching Lisa and Courtney to a lab, I could not measure another prerequisite, their maximum aerobic capacity. I also could not measure a third prerequisite (equally critical for success) not mentioned by Shorten: how they, or the others, might respond to training—both physically and psychologically.

Shorten identified economical runners as those able to "show smaller changes in the body's mechanical energy during the running stride and also a greater degree of energy transfer between and within the body's parts." In other words, they run smoothly. You don't need a coach's eye to determine that some runners run more smoothly than others any more than you need a coach's eye to spot whether a quarterback can throw a spiral pass. Ideally, you want a pass that is both well thrown and well aimed.

The same is true in running. Jerky running form requires more mechanical energy and therefore incurs a physiological cost, according to Shorten. This is the equivalent of the wobbly pass. For example, some runners bound across the ground, pumping their arms to lift themselves off the track with each lengthening stride. They supplement leg power with arm power and thus move very swiftly for short periods of time. Over short distances, sheer strength can overcome what seem to be serious form faults. Many fast sprinters are not pretty runners. One example is Bob Hayes, winner of the 100 meters at the 1964 Olympic Games and later a wide receiver for the Dallas Cowboys. Regardless of Hayes's form, he was very effective while running fast, either to get to the finish line or to get to where he could catch passes. But while powerful arm and leg movements may be efficient at short distances, jerky movements interfere with speed for the long run, where style often overcomes strength.

The girls who had beaten Lisa and Courtney had more strength than style. They were runners in the Bob Hayes mold, fast over short distances. Inevitably, as race distances lengthen, smooth striders run past them. But some runners have neither strength nor style. Shorten admitted that trying to turn inefficient runners into smooth striders was not easy. He did suggest two possibilities.

First, lack of flexibility restricts range of movement and may limit economy. Thus, runners interested in improving form should first improve their flexibility. This is why so many coaches stress stretching drills, a subject covered in chapter 4.

Second, Shorten added that jerky movements incur an energy cost without contributing to efficient propulsion. "In coach's terms," he summarized, "an efficient running action will appear to be smooth, relaxed, and rangy—but you don't need a computer to tell you that." Converting jerky movements into smooth movements also is no easy task, but it's one that sometimes can be accomplished with the use of speed drills, a subject covered in chapter 7.

Had Shorten visited Michigan City, I may have introduced him to Lisa and Courtney. Or I could have told him about Curt Stone, the epitome of an economical runner.

Stone attended Pennsylvania State University and later competed for the New York Athletic Club. He was America's premiere distance runner when I first became involved in track-and-field. He placed sixth in the 1948 Olympic 5000. I was still in high school then, but four years later, I ran against him at the 1952 Olympic Trials in California, where he won the 10,000 and set an American record. Later I watched as he also won the 5000 and set another American record.

Of all the dozen or so runners on the Los Angeles Coliseum track that day, Curt Stone easily was the smoothest. He moved along the surface with minimum effort, his inevitable triumph seemingly preordained by his ability, whether practiced or God-given, to run with economy of style. Of course, Stone didn't win every race—no runner does. In fact, at the Olympics in Helsinki, he lost decisively to Zatopek—the man who moved like a maniac. Even then, I continued to admire him.

But my story does not end there. A half dozen years later, at a meet in which I ran well, a track aficionado approached me and asked, "Do you know who you look like when you run?" I replied, "Who?" To my surprise, he said, "Curt Stone!"

Did I run like Stone because after that day in the Coliseum, I modeled my running after him? Or did I merely *think* he ran better because I already realized, at least subconsciously, that I ran like him?

## SHORTER STRIDES, FASTER FINISH

I recalled another runner from my past: Jim Beatty, one of the world's best 5000-meter runners in the early 1960s and later a TV commentator. Beatty is now a member of The Athletics Congress Hall of Fame, but in 1956, the two of us were unheralded members of an American track team that spent three weeks training and competing in Finland. During a workout one afternoon at Suomi Urheilupisto, a sports camp near the town of Vierumaki, Finnish coach Armas Valste watched Beatty run an interval workout. Beatty was relatively short and stocky, but he had a long, flowing stride that allowed him to swallow long stretches of ground in large gulps. Valste observed him and commented tersely: "He overstrides!"

At the time, Beatty was still attending the University of North Carolina and had a mile best of about 4:07. He graduated and retired from the sport. Then, while watching the U.S./Soviet track meet on television a few years later, he wondered how good he could become if he fully dedicated himself to excellence. He moved to Los Angeles to train under Mihaly Igloi, the former Hungarian Olympic coach who had defected to the United States in 1956. Igloi placed Beatty on a twice-daily, 100-mile-a-week program that consisted almost entirely of interval work on the track.

I next saw Beatty in 1959 during the telecast of an indoor mile race, and my first reaction was that he had cut his stride length in half. In actuality, he probably had sliced only inches from it, but it appeared to be a short, quick-tempo, efficient running style, well suited to his height. He employed this short stride for maybe 10 of the 11 laps that made up the mile race. Then, almost as though he had shifted gears, he began a powerful, long-striding sprint that swept him past his opponents. He won that day in 3:59, a considerable improvement over his college time—and in an era when sub–4-minute miles still remained a rarity.

Beatty had shown me that you can improve your running form to make it more efficient. Whether this improvement had come from a conscious manipulation of style by his coach or from an unconscious reaction by Beatty's body for protection during an exhausting training regimen, I don't know. His shift mirrored my own experience in seeing my stride length shorten as I went from 25 miles a week in college to 100 miles a week several years later.

# A POINT-BY-POINT ANALYSIS

In an effort to answer some questions about my form, I once visited the Nike Sport Research Laboratory to be analyzed by a team of scientists that included at that time E. C. (Ned) Frederick, Ph.D., and Dr. Jack Daniels. This was in the early 1980s, when Nike operated a research facility at its factory in Exeter, New Hampshire. Dr. Frederick was in charge of the group, whose mission was to determine what makes runners run faster and how this could be applied to the manufacture of better running shoes.

That day, they carefully studied my economy of motion. Dr. Frederick planned a series of tests that utilized a treadmill, a force plate, and cameras. I was photographed from all angles; then the film was quickly developed and examined on a digital analysis machine. Before the tests began, the lab crew marked black dots on various parts of my body, particularly on each joint, so the machine could plot my running form.

The first tests consisted of 6-minute treadmill runs at various paces: 6:30, 6:00, 5:30, and 5:00. Near the middle of each run, I was photographed from both the front and back. These photos, taken at 200 frames per minute, showed how my feet, legs, and joints reacted to the tiny collisions that came with each running step. Midway through each run, I donned a mouthpiece connected to a gas analyzer that monitored my breathing and determined, by the volume of oxygen I burned, how efficiently I ran. At the end of the final run at a 5-minute pace, Dr. Daniels tilted the treadmill 1 degree every minute, forcing me to sprint faster to stay on. This way, he was able to measure my $VO_2$ max. I managed to stay on the treadmill until it was tilted to 2 degrees; then I begged for mercy. At that point, I was running nearly a 4:40 pace and hyperventilating in my unsuccessful attempt to convince my muscles to accept more oxygen. That was the sign that I had reached my $VO_2$ max. Dr. Daniels recorded my $VO_2$ max at 66.4 ml/kg/min, giving him a benchmark to compare the efficiency of my other runs.

After the treadmill tests, I moved to a rubberized runway that extended the length of the building. Two force plates were embedded in its middle. My task was to run at various paces—again from 6:30 to 5:00—across one of the plates, as a long jumper might attempt to hit a takeoff board. The plate recorded my footstrike, which revealed valuable information about my running efficiency. It told me how hard I landed, where on my foot I landed, and how I pushed off. Research assistant Tom Clark also photographed me from the side during these force plate runs, so he could measure my range of actions, including my stride length, at the same time.

Later that afternoon, I returned to the treadmill for more tests, designed to measure the relative efficiency of running with or without orthotics. Finally, returning the next morning, I did five more runs at a 5:30 pace, but with varying stride lengths to determine the efficiency of my natural stride, measured by Clark the previous day. To guide me in varying my stride length, Dr. Daniels set a metronome beside the treadmill. In order to move to its rhythm, I either had to quicken my pace by shortening my stride or slow my pace by lengthening my stride.

Thus, the scientists probed my form.

## BEWARE OF MAGIC FORMULAS

After all the gadgets were taken off of me and the tests were completed, I felt a little anxious and curious. Like most runners, I'm always interested in any hot tip or secret method that would reduce my race times by a few seconds. I wandered now and then into a side room where several of the research assistants were digitizing the films they made of me. They would freeze one frame and twist knobs to manipulate cross hairs, horizontal and vertical, over the various dots on my legs and shoes. A push of the button entered data into the computer. "You're symmetrical," they informed me after a careful study of the films. I pronate somewhat, more with the left foot than the right, but I do not have a rear-foot control problem.

I asked them to run the film in slow motion. My straight-ahead stride was quite apparent now. No obvious technical flaws showed. It is one reason why I have had relatively few injuries during more than four decades of running. Nevertheless, despite my stride's relative smoothness, I was shocked to see the impact when my foot collided with the ground and the reverberating reactions of my leg muscles. If this is what happens to an efficient and symmetrical runner, how do any of us survive a run of more than a few miles? The body is a remarkable machine.

Prior to my lab visit, Dr. Frederick measured another runner whose profile was very similar to mine. A student at a New England university, this young runner weighed almost the same as I, was about an inch taller, and had a $VO_2$ max of 70.3, about equal to my best when I was younger but higher than what mine was at the time of the tests. Still, he ran 2 miles almost a minute slower than I did. Dr. Frederick explained that the reason for the discrepancy was that this strong, talented runner was inefficient.

In order to analyze just what constitutes my efficient form, Dr. Frederick compared my film with the young runner's. The key difference was clear. It was what we call vertical displacement—that is, how high off the ground a runner raises himself with each stride. This is where the greatest energy cost in running comes from, so the lower you can run without tripping, the better. At the peak of my stride, I raised myself only 6.5 centimeters. The other runner lifted himself 7.8 centimeters. On a metric ruler, that extra 1.3 centimeters doesn't seem like much, but Clark described it as a "meaningful difference." With my lower stride, I spent much less time in the air (a full 30 milliseconds), transmitted 10 percent less force to the ground, and used 9 percent less energy when running the same 5:30 pace. This all added up to a short, efficient stride that made the important difference between our 2-mile times.

In the jargon of the laboratory, I had a "quick turnover time," aided in part by a quick braking motion on my arm backswing that permitted me to thrust my legs forward rapidly. Joan Benoit Samuelson also had quick turnover. The two of us, at least in 1981, were closely matched in several values, including $VO_2$ max, stride rate, and race times. "We should put the two of you up on side-by-side treadmills and see how you perform," Clark suggested. (Samuelson, of course, would get faster, while I simply got older.)

My stride rate was 103 cycles, or 206 footsteps, per minute. Samuelson's stride rate was 100 cycles per minute. In a classic study at Dr. Ken Cooper's Institute for Aerobic Research in Dallas in 1974, the stride rates of elite runners at a 5:30 pace were measured at 95 cycles per minute. Further, their stride lengths were 165 percent of their leg length, from crotch to heel. A group of merely "good" runners measured 172 percent, almost the same as our young New England student. In contrast, my stride length measured 146 percent, significantly shorter than the Dallas elite.

Was it possible that my stride length actually was too short? Maybe. The standardized test required me to run on a steadily moving treadmill in rhythm with a metronome, which forced me to adjust my stride. I ran five 6-minute tests at a 5:30 pace with stride rates chosen randomly: 93, 113, 98, 108, and finally my normal rate, 103. At 93, I felt as though I was bounding, floating in air between steps. At 113, I had to move my legs so rapidly that it took intense concentration to stay on the beat. I felt comfortable at 98, less so at 108, but most relaxed at my customary 103.

Yet when we measured the volume of oxygen I consumed during each run to examine my efficiency, I discovered that

I consumed 3,816 and 3,818 milliliters per minute at cadences of 98 and 103. I was most efficient (3,783 milliliters per minute) while bounding along at 93 cycles per minute. Apparently, I might run even more efficiently than I already do if I lengthened my stride. Maybe if I worked more on flexibility and utilized bounding drills, I could become a better runner.

Should I modify my style? Dr. Frederick shook his head. "There's probably a very good reason why you run the way you do," he said. "Even though you may lose some efficiency, you're probably protecting yourself from injury and putting less strain on your muscles by staying close to the ground. I wouldn't change. The main thing we learn as we do more biomechanical research is how abysmally ignorant we are. We really don't know what makes some people run faster than others. I would beware of people who claim to have magic formulas."

# THE FIVE ELEMENTS OF EFFICIENT FORM

So what is good running form? And how do you recognize it? Fred Wilt, a contemporary of Curt Stone, made an interesting analysis of running form in a book he produced for the Canadian Track & Field Association, *The Complete Canadian Runner*. Some of Wilt's views are included in this list of five elements of form and how efficient runners use them. How do you stack up?

**Footstrike:** Most better runners land on their midfoot, that is, at a point just behind the ball of the foot. They then drop down on their heel, and their body glides above a foot that is planted firmly on the ground before they push off with the toes. Some land more forward on the ball (toe runners), others land more flat-footed (heel runners). Different runners have different plants, dictated by how the parts of their body fit together, otherwise known as biomechanics. If you possess an imperfect footplant (which can cause injury), you may need to see a podiatrist for orthotic inserts, although most runners can control such problems by carefully selecting shoes. The worst you can do to your footstrike is to try to adjust your landing to accommodate what you think other runners do.

**Stride length:** There is no definition of a "perfect" stride length; The best stride lengths depend on each runner's natural form. In general, however, a short, quick-tempo stride may be more economical in a 5-K or 10-K race. A long stride causes the runner to lose momentum and waste energy by pushing too far ahead of his center of gravity—thus, the term *overstriding*. But understriding can be just as great a sin.

**Carriage:** Your trunk should be more or less perpendicular to the ground, and your hips should be forward. American Olympian Garry Bjorklund once told me: "Novice runners have a tendency to sit down, to put their weight behind them. They need to bring their center of gravity forward and get their weight over their metatarsals [the part of your foot between the ankle and the toes]."

**Arm carry:** Your arms should move in rhythm with your legs. They should swing forward more than sideways, with your elbows in and your hands cupped (rather than clenched). Bill Bowerman, retired track coach for the University of Oregon, liked to have his runners carry their arms high across the chest. Villanova's Jumbo Elliott wanted his runners to carry their arms low, "thumbs in their pockets." If these two renowned coaches can differ as to what is proper form, then there may be *no* proper form.

**Head position:** The head serves as keystone for the rest of the body. Back in some paleolithic era, a coach once told me to fix my gaze 10 yards up the track and use my eyes to anchor my head in a relaxed position. That is probably as good advice as any. If you allow your eyes, and gaze, to wander all over the road, you probably will wander with them.

# HIDDEN FORM FLAWS OF THE ELITE

I wonder how much even the most experienced coach can learn about a runner's form merely by observing with the naked eye. During my visit to the Nike Sport Research Laboratory, I observed Samuelson running on the treadmill. From the side, her legs seemed a blur as she used 200 steps a minute to run at a 6-minute pace. I could tell little by observing her from different angles. She *seemed* to move very smoothly, another Curt Stone.

Yet Dr. Frederick, standing next to me, pointed out that Samuelson favored her right leg, the result of a leg broken while skiing years before. He knew because they had analyzed her style by camera and computer. That was three years before Samuelson strode into history with her victory in the first Olympic marathon for women, at Los Angeles in 1984. But it also was three years before a severe knee injury, perhaps caused by the imbalance detected by Dr. Frederick, forced her to have surgery that almost caused her to miss the Olympics.

Dr. Frederick told me that when they test various individuals, they sometimes discover that runners who appear to have the worst form are judged most efficient in the laboratory. By now it is common knowledge, for example, that Bill Rodgers, for all his other virtues, has a strange right arm swing that compensates for a slight foot imbalance. And Frank Shorter swings his left arm outward, so you do not want to pass him on that side for fear of getting struck. Dr. Frederick said that Tony Sandoval, winner of the 1980 Olympic Trials marathon, functioned like two separate runners in the area of footstrike: flat-footed on the left, a classic midstrike on the right.

Woe to the coach who would have attempted to modify their forms. In the closing stages of a race, they move with the relentless energy of the stone ball rolling down the chute toward Indiana Jones.

During another project, the scientists at Nike Sport Research Laboratory tested footstrikes by having a group of good runners adjust their form during different runs on the treadmill—one time landing on the balls of their feet, another time midfoot, another time more flat-footed, and once, even on their heels. They expected to discover that the midfoot landing was most efficient, since film and force plate analysis suggests that the world's fastest runners run that way.

During the tests, most of the runners found landing on their heels to be least comfortable. One subject described heel running during the test as a truly horrible experience, akin to Chinese water torture. Yet when the results were computed, heel running proved most efficient, even for that one reluctant subject. "Sometimes the more you learn, the more you realize how little you know," Dr. Frederick admits. He cautioned runners against using this one experiment to justify a major shift in their running style. "There may be other reasons, beyond what we can measure easily in a laboratory, why a runner should stick with a particular style," he warns.

# AN INVENTORY OF FORM ENHANCERS

Let me offer not necessarily a magic formula but rather some suggestions as to how you might at least be aware of your running form, if not improve it. In his article in *Running Research News,* Dr. Anderson quoted several techniques used by Dr. Daniels to improve running form: interval training, downhill running, uphill running, and bounding drills. I've devoted a chapter to each of these techniques. But for now, let's briefly discuss how to use these drills to enhance your form.

Interval training has been proven as a way of improving running ability. It can strengthen you aerobically and anaerobically. It can strengthen your legs. It can strengthen your confidence. I've always felt that one of the greatest values of interval training is that it strengthened my ability to concentrate. It permitted me to maintain good form. During interval sessions at the beginning of the season, I would often find my mind drifting and my form lagging in the backstretch. As weeks went on and I became more comfortable with the training routine, I found I could concentrate and maintain an efficient form for the full lap. Maintaining peak efficiency over a longer period of time inevitably helped me to run faster. My times would improve not merely in workouts but also in races.

Dr. Daniels apparently agrees, suggesting to Dr. Anderson that runners should combine short work bouts of 400 meters, carried out at a rapid (but not maximum) velocity, with maximum rest: a work-to-rest ratio of 1 to 4, or greater. That is, for each ¼ mile you run in 75 seconds, you should rest 5 minutes or more. "The idea is to be completely rested and refreshed for every 400-meter run," Dr. Anderson writes, "so that you can maintain good running form throughout."

Dr. Daniels also recommended downhill running to become accustomed to running faster by increasing your leg turnover without increasing your effort. He suggested slight downhills—no more than 2 percent grade—preferably on golf fairways. Uphill running, on the other hand, is used to improve the power of the buttocks muscles, getting them more involved in the motion of running and forcing you to use more effort. "The idea is not to sprint, but to move steadily," Dr. Daniels says. Bounding drills, championed by coach Bell, similarly improve strength, flexibility, and running form.

Apart from what the experts say, I'm convinced that runners need to develop what Bell calls body awareness and what I call a feel for form. You need to become aware of how your body moves as you run. One way of achieving that is to attend a running camp where you can be videotaped, so that you can see what you look like running. Or if you own a video camera, you can have someone else videotape you. Unfortunately, you won't be able to digitize those motions as they did in Dr. Frederick's lab, but you can at least get an idea of how you run.

With that picture of yourself running, try the following form drills.

**Run barefoot in the park.** On a summer day, go to the beach or golf course and find a smooth stretch of sand or fairway. Remove your shoes. Jog or run at a comfortable pace for a distance of about 50 or 100 meters. Can you feel the point where your foot contacts the ground? Do you land midfoot or more toward the toe or heel? Can you run more

# TEN TIPS ON RUNNING FORM

Fred Wilt was a distance runner on the 1948 and 1952 U.S. Olympic teams and became famous for his legendary indoor mile encounters at that time with Wisconsin's Don Gehrmann. After retiring from the FBI, Wilt coached the women's running teams at Purdue University. He edited the publication *Track Technique* and advised various athletes, including 1964 Olympian Buddy Edelen, who once held the world marathon record of 2:14:28. Wilt currently lives in Anderson, Indiana. The following information related to running form is excerpted from a book he produced for the Canadian Track & Field Association, *The Complete Canadian Runner*.

1. Running form is a completely individual issue. Each athlete differs from every other at least to a minute extent in height, weight, bone structure, length and size of muscles, point of muscle origin and insertion, strength, flexibility, posture, and personality, in addition to numerous other features. Therefore, no two runners should ever use identical form, even though they all adhere to basic mechanical principles.

2. It is a form error of the highest magnitude to run without permitting the heel to touch and rest on the ground with each stride, without reservation, in a ball-heel grounding action. This is true at all running speeds, especially sprinting.

3. It is physically possible to land heel-first in running, but this is quite incorrect and almost never seen, since it jars the body excessively and can be done only at very slow running speeds. Landing heel-first and

comfortably by adjusting your footstrike? Probably not, but at least you will be aware of your landing. Running gently on the grass is one way to develop body awareness. Running on wet sand and studying your footprints is another.

**Run fast at the track.** Visit a 400-meter track. Begin at the starting line for the 300 meters, at the head of the "toe running" (refusing to permit the heels to ground) are both incorrect.

4. Ideally, the position of the feet in running is one in which the inner borders fall approximately along a straight line. Athletes should run *in* a straight line, but not necessarily *on* such a line. When one foot is placed directly in front of the other, lateral (sideways) balance is impaired.

5. Runners in races longer than sprint distance wherein economy of energy is the paramount consideration should use a natural stride: not exaggerated, not long, not short, but of a length in keeping with maximum economy of effort for the running speed required.

6. Both understriding and overstriding are faults. Each runner has his own optimum stride length at any given speed, depending upon leg length, muscular strength, and joint flexibility.

7. At uniform top speed with zero acceleration, if the athlete was running in a vacuum with no wind resistance, there would be no body lean at all.

8. The hands should be carried in a relaxed, cupped position at all running speeds. They should never be rigidly clenched in a fist while running, since this produces tension, which causes unnecessary fatigue.

9. The head should be aligned naturally with the trunk, and the eyes should be focused a few meters ahead while running.

10. Usually the best solution to apparent form problems is many repetitions of running short distances, such as 100 meters, at a fast, though not exhausting, pace.

back straightaway, and slowly accelerate throughout that straightaway until you are running near race pace through the turn. As you come into the home straightaway, continue your acceleration to top speed at the line. What happens to your form during this acceleration run? At what point and pace do you become a more efficient, or less efficient, runner? Focus on what happens to your knee lift, your stride length, your posture, your arm carry, your head angle. At what point does fatigue cause your running form to deteriorate? Trot out the video camera again if it helps you answer these questions.

**Run straight on the road.** Pick a road (hopefully low-traffic) where you can follow a straight line: a painted stripe in the center, a crack in the pavement, or the separation between pavement and shoulder. Run at a steady race pace for a distance of ½ mile or more. Focus your attention on that line. Think of yourself as a machine moving along it, like a train on a rail. Can you run straight along it without wavering back and forth? Is your head straight, are your eyes level? Are your arms moving smoothly back and forth, in rhythm with your legs? Are your legs moving straight forward and kicking straight back?

**Run focused in a race.** Entering your next 5-K or 10-K, try to concentrate completely on your running movements. Can you ignore the scenery, the sights and sounds of the race around you? Can you run without talking? Are you only peripherally aware of other runners around you? Can you maintain the form you practiced on the grass, on the track, on the road? You may need to do so if you want to maximize your ability to run fast.

# Chapter 6

# DYNAMIC FLEXIBILITY

## UNUSUAL DRILLS WITH REMARKABLE RESULTS

**R**oy Benson, an Atlanta fitness consultant, stands before a group of several hundred teenagers jammed into the bleachers of a gymnasium in North Carolina. They are high school cross-country runners spending a week at his Florida Running Camp (so named because Benson started it while track coach at the University of Florida). The high schoolers have come to camp to become better runners. With the week of hard training at Benson's camp, plus the knowledge gained, they hope to return home with skills not possessed by their rivals.

You may be wondering what you can learn from a group of high school runners. Plenty. Benson's advice applies to any runner looking for speed.

Today's lesson is *dynamic flexibility*—although Benson does not call it by that name, or by other familiar terms like plyometrics, ballistic stretching, or speed drills. Dynamic flexibility is a form of stretching—a means of getting loose—that involves continuous movement, as opposed to the static nature of regular stretching.

At his camp, Benson offers what he describes as "learn-by-doing drills." He promises the runners: "These drills are going to teach you how to get stronger, how to be more flexible, how to be more coordinated." Soon he has them out of the bleachers and lined up facing him on the wide side of the gym.

Benson concedes that one way for runners to improve their speed is to increase their running distance: "If you're running 20 miles a week, I'll guarantee that if you can move up to 40, you'll run faster." But one problem as runners increase distance, he continues, is that they often *decrease* flexibility: "The first thing that happens is that your hamstrings get tight, because you're using this short stride. Your calves get tight, your shins get tight, your quads get tight. You develop *in*flexibility, resulting in a shorter and shorter range of motion, and pretty soon, you can't run as fast." Benson states that runners must continue to fight this tightening process by using flexibility drills.

Another factor, Benson explains, is that by not working the muscles used when you run fast, those muscles weaken and compound the problem. Finally, says Benson, runners who run long also run very erect, landing toward the rear of their feet, on their heels. That may be an economical way to run distance, but not to run fast. For speed, runners need to learn to land further forward on their feet—more midfoot, toward their toes.

Benson asks those at his camp to run in place. Soon the gym thunders with the sound of thumping shoes.

This is the first step in learning flexibility: employing simple movements that will help you loosen up. There are, of course, different approaches. In fact, a generation of runners has been taught that the best way is to stretch in a static position. "Don't bounce!" is a warning offered by almost every stretching expert, including Bob Anderson.

He writes: "Holding a stretch as far as you can go or bouncing up and down strains the muscles and activates the stretch reflex. These harmful methods cause pain, as well as physical damage due to the microscopic tearing of muscle fibers."

Good advice, but static stretching is not the only way to loosen up. Fast running is another way. Simply by sprinting out and lengthening your stride, you stretch your muscles. Of course, you have to be loose to run fast, so it becomes a question of which comes first, the chicken or the egg, the stretch or the stride? The truth is that dynamic flexibility drills do not replace static stretching. Rather, they often work well together.

# *HIGH KNEES*

"Stop!" Benson yells out to his class, and he asks how many were landing on their heels. Nobody raises a hand. Benson nods and explains that it is impossible to run in place landing on your heels.

Benson again asks them to run in place—but to now begin moving forward gradually, across the gym. The campers comply and, in so doing, learn one of the first drills, what I call high knees. In this drill, runners thrust their knees upward vigorously, counterbalancing with powerful arm pumps. It's more like sprinting in place than running in place.

As the campers move from one side of the gym to the other, Benson instructs: "Stay up on your toes! Get that feel. Feel yourself coming down on your midfoot, the ball of your foot. That's the feeling you want when you run fast."

To emphasize the high-knee aspect of the drill, Benson next has the high schoolers hold their hands out in front of them, just higher than their knees. Jogging back across the floor, they hit their hands with their knees, gradually raising their hands and lifting their knees to waist-high.

"One of the side benefits of these drills is to turn you into better athletes," he says. "We want to make you feel more comfortable and coordinated when you sprint." Benson notes that high-knee drills are good for strengthening the hip flexors, which he identifies as the most important running muscle in your body. "The only way you strengthen your hip flexors," he says, "is to run up hills or stadium steps, or do speedwork—or do drills such as this." He advises running drills when you're fresh, not when you're fatigued from a hard workout.

A variation on high knees is a less dynamic drill I call the drum major. Instead of running in place, it is more like walking in place. The motion is the same. You rise up on one toe, thrusting the opposite knee as high up toward your chest as possible, using a vigorous arm pump to achieve this. But you walk rather than jog or run. You don't leave the ground, so it's a safe drill if you're recovering from a minor injury. I also recommend the drum major as a good introductory drill for older runners who have just begun to get acquainted with dynamic flexibility drills in an attempt to improve their running. Masters (or beginning) runners can begin with the drum major as a prelude to high knees. But don't abandon it once you've learned the more dynamic drills. It remains a good flexibility drill for all ages and levels.

A complementary static exercise to high knees or the drum major is the knee pull. Stand in place, and with both hands, pull one knee to your chest, stretching your hamstring. While warming up before a race, I sometimes use all three drills—knee pull, drum major, and high knees—to loosen my muscles.

Still another variation is to do the knee pull while lying on your back, a stretch I included in the warm-up routine described in chapter 4. (See page 38.)

I also use the knee pull while soaking in a hot whirlpool. It's one of my favorite stretches, mainly because I constantly must fight the tendency of my hamstrings to tighten during long runs. Most distance runners have tight hamstrings; they come with the territory. It's one reason why we have trouble touching our toes.

# *HIGH HEELS*

High knees is perhaps the easiest flexibility drill to learn and practice. But Benson now moves to the next drill, what he calls the fanny-flicker and what I call high heels. Coaches sometimes call it the butt-kicker. I sometimes refer to it as the glute-kicker, as in gluteus maximus.

Benson begins by walking his group through the drill, on their toes: "As you go farther and farther, lift your heels higher and higher, until you're kicking your fanny." Leaning forward makes the exercise easier to learn, although I recommend an upright posture for more practiced butt-kickers. Once Benson's campers learn the movement in slow motion, he brings them butt-kicking back across the gym. "Nice and slowly," says Benson. "Short steps. The minute you try to go fast, it gets too challenging and you fall apart. Short steps. *Flick! Flick! Flick!*"

Benson nudges me and points toward two girls—sprinters, as it turns out. "Watch their kick," says Benson. "They get perfect full extension across the front of their ankles. Their toes point. The classic back kick. That, to me, is the secret of speed."

Indeed, one way to judge a runner's speed is by watching him or her do these drills. On one of my cross-country teams, two runners clearly drilled better than the others. Had you sent that team across the grass in one of the above drills, you would immediately have noticed Don Pearce and Liz Galaviz. Don qualified for the state championships in his junior and senior years by running the 800 meters in 1:57. Liz, a talented sophomore, was the best half-miler on the girls' squad; she ran 2:32 to qualify for sectionals.

Ironically, Don was perhaps the least flexible runner on the team, so static stretching was very difficult for him. And because he didn't like to be seen doing poorly in any activity, he did his stretching routine very reluctantly. If

Don had a fault (shared by many runners), it was his tendency to rely on his natural ability. Would Don have become an even faster runner had he paid more attention to improving his flexibility? I'm inclined to think so, although scientists offer no proof.

Benson explains to his class that high heels is good for stretching the hamstrings but is particularly good for stretching the quadriceps. "You've got to relax your quads to get that heel up," he instructs. For older, beginning, or injured runners, walking in place with the high-heel motion works quite nicely. As a complementary static stretch for this drill, try the heel hold. (See page 36.)

# SKIPPING

High knees and high heels are great for beginners. They require relatively little skill or flexibility. Trickier is Benson's next set of drills, which involves skipping. He teaches two variations: skipping for height, and skipping for distance, in which you try to cover as much ground as possible.

Both varieties are extremely dynamic and involve all of the major muscles used in running fast. Thus, skipping is the heart of the art of dynamic flexibility. In fact, one value of all that goes before—from static stretching to high knees and high heels—is that you become loose enough to do this dynamic exercise. There is no single stretch that complements skipping, although it might be said that all stretches do just that.

Many runners have difficulty learning skipping drills at first, even though most of us skipped naturally as young children. Perhaps it's just a matter of practicing it again. When my oldest son, Kevin, appeared for cross-country practice at Indiana University, he kept getting his legs crossed when coach Sam Bell taught the I.U. team the drill. Kevin eventually went behind the dormitory one Sunday morning and practiced skipping until he learned the rhythm. If you have problems learning to skip again, don't feel embarrassed. With some practice, you *can* master this skill. Kevin did, and it helped him finish the season as the second-fastest runner on the I.U. team that won the Big Ten title and placed eighth at the NCAA championships. The only runner faster than he was Olympian Jim Spivey.

As Benson sends his campers skipping across the gym, sure enough, one lad keeps getting legs and arms tangled. Arm movements in skipping are like arm movements in running or walking: the left arm comes up as the right knee comes up, and so forth. But the camper keeps getting his left arm and left knee up together, until finally, everything falls apart. Benson sends him back and forth across the floor several times, but the camper just can't seem to pick up the right rhythm.

It's not easy. So Benson instructs his students on the technique of skipping: "To skip, you must be coordinated. You start skipping with high knees, stay relaxed, and slowly bring your arms in like a sprinter. Arms are straight, pointing down the track, not across your body. You want to have straight hands, up about jaw height, so you're pumping your arms, getting up in the air. I want to see you hanging like Michael Jordan! Pump your arms. Elbows go as high as possible in the back. That helps you push harder against the ground with that opposite toe. Then come up in the front with a short punching motion to help you lift in the air. Now let's try it slowly. Everybody together, doing a little skip with your arms up. Get those knees high! Hang up there!"

Admittedly, skipping is not easy to explain—or teach. You just do it. If you *think* too much about what you're doing, it may confuse you more. One way to learn to skip is to make very slow and short movements at first: Skip a few inches forward on one foot, then the other. Hold both hands in front of you for balance. Gradually let your hands counterbalance your foot movements. Then stretch out. Once you learn to skip, you'll be amazed how simple—and fun—the exercise becomes.

As I mentioned earlier, there are two variations on the skipping drill: skipping for height, and skipping for distance.

Skipping for height is akin to high knees. You move forward gradually, concentrating on getting high off the ground. Accentuate your knee rise. Counterbalance with your arms. As one knee comes up high, the opposite arm thrusts skyward in a palm-open movement. Don't try to cover too much ground. When my team does skipping for height, I yell at any of my runners who try to "win" the drill by moving ahead of the others. Getting up in the air is most important. Indeed, those doing the best job with this exercise are often in the back rather than the front.

Skipping for distance is similar in its movements, only now you try to cover distance horizontally rather than vertically. The knees and arms still come up high, but movement is more forward. I still discourage those who try to "win" the drill, since moving forward too rapidly makes the skipping too difficult to maintain.

Skipping drills are best done on smooth, soft surfaces. Football fields are sometimes too lumpy for safe practice of this or any other drill in this chapter. The tracks around them often are too hard. Basketball courts are okay, since the wood floor offers some bounce. The perfect surface is the fairway of a golf course—if you can avoid being evicted by the greenkeepers. In summer months, when days are long, I'll often arrive at the golf course at sunrise, hours before the golfers and greenkeepers.

# TOE WALK

As his campers skip back and forth across the gym floor, Benson talks to me about speed: "When you go to sprint, you don't care about economy. You don't care how smooth and relaxed you are. You want to be powerful, dynamic. You pump your arms to make your strides go faster. You turn over quicker. That way, you'll really take off."

Benson has one final drill to teach his campers: the toe walk, a less dynamic variation of the drum major discussed on page 68. It's a good exercise for calf muscles—and a simple one. All you need to do is walk forward and accentuate your toe push-off: rolling up and over on the toes of the feet. "Way up on your toes," says Benson. "Don't bounce.

Walk. Stay up on your toes. Feel your calves tightening. You're building power, strength, explosion."

Having used nearly an hour to teach four simple drills (high knees, high heels, skipping for height and for distance, and toe walks), Benson releases the group to its next activities. Had he the time or the inclination, Benson could have offered several additional speed drills. One book I own—*Plyometrics: Explosive Power Training* by James C. Radcliffe and Robert C. Farentinos—offers *dozens* of drills, some involving steps and medicine balls. One illustration shows a coach telling his athlete to jump off a cliff. Going off the edge, the athlete asks: "Are you *sure*, Coach, this is how to do plyometrics?"

Indeed, beginning runners may feel as though they hit hard at the bottom of the cliff the day after their first dynamic flexibility drills. Any time you use different (untrained) muscles, you probably will feel sore for 24 to 72 hours afterward, and it makes little difference how well trained you are as a runner. The same would happen if you switched suddenly to cycling or skiing or tennis. For this reason, introduce bounding drills *very* gradually into your program. Begin with only one or two drills and minimal repetitions. Do them on your easy days. Gradually introduce additional drills and increase the number of repetitions. You will avoid both discomfort and the increased risk of injury that comes as the price for wanting to run fast.

## *FAST FEET*

One additional drill that I use with my team is fast feet. It's one that I learned from now-retired University of Oregon coach Bill Bowerman. I consider Bowerman to have been the single most influential American coach in the area of training distance runners. I'm not alone in that assessment.

While giving me an interview for an article, Bowerman described a drill he had learned from the previous Oregon coach, Bill Hayward. The drill is very simple, similar to high knees, except that instead of raising your knees high, you keep them low and move your feet as rapidly as you can: *Pop! Pop! Pop! Pop!* The arms move equally fast in short arcs.

But that wasn't the only thing I learned. I couldn't help but take advantage of Bowerman's expertise. So I asked him, "What are the secrets of running fast—if that isn't too basic a question?"

"No, it's a good question," he said. "I did an article with somebody once on the secrets of speed. It was published in *Sports Illustrated* in 1968. And basically I was telling what Hayward taught me. It's very elemental: A straight line is the shortest distance between two points. My line mechanics were so bad that my foot would fly out to the side. One of the things that Hayward had me do was lean up against a wall and watch my feet. I would bring my leg through like this to try to get the feel of my leg moving in a straight line. [Bowerman leaned against his fireplace and slowly rotated his leg to mimic a sprinter's stride.] One leg, then the other. I've done this with a lot of people, and it works.

"The second thing was reaction time. [He jogged in place, his feet pitter-pattering at a rapid pace.] You stand like this and gradually speed up your legs. . . . The reaction of bouncing the feet rapidly, then bringing the knees up slowly, trying to keep everything straight ahead, picking up the rhythm—but you don't do it only with the legs. You have to use the arms, because that's the way you're wired. By gradually speeding up the arms, you speed up the legs. Then use the sprint distances as merely a measure of testing; how much is this fellow improving? We do sprint drills three times a week. High knee, fast leg, and sprint 40 yards. Simple drills: everything straight ahead, reaction time, mechanics of running. If there's some bad habit, work on it. For every action, there's an equal and opposite reaction.

"That was what Hayward did for me. I never knew how fast I was. I couldn't beat anybody; I was the slowest man on the high school team. After Hayward was through with me, the only man I couldn't beat was our university sprinter, Paul Starr, who was third in the National AAU Championships . . ."

"So you were able to improve the speed of your sprinters with these simple drills of Bill Hayward's," I said.

"And what works for sprinters applies to other runners as well," he explained. "God determines how fast you're going to run; I can help only with the mechanics."

Bowerman's successor as track coach at Oregon, Bill Dellinger, later described the fast-foot drill in an article in *Runner's World:* "The concept behind this is to see how fast you can make your feet move. Unlike the high-knees drill, you barely lift your knees at all. The emphasis is on quickness. Don't stride out. Simply move your feet as if you were running over hot coals. You're teaching your feet to react quickly."

## *TWO ADVANCED DRILLS*

There are two additional drills that my son Kevin learned from coach Bell at Indiana University that are worth mentioning. However, I don't necessarily recommend them for all (particularly older) runners, because of the stress they place on the joints. These drills are bounding and the double leg hop.

Bounding is an elongated running action in which you concentrate on lifting your knees and pumping with your arms up. This is not running. You bound. You hop from one leg to the other: left, right, left, right, getting as high off the ground as you can. Focus on your knee lift. Add this to your repertoire of flexibility drills only after you are well practiced in the other drills and your leg muscles have adapted to what is admittedly a very vigorous exercise.

The double leg hop also is not a drill for inexperienced runners. The movement is similar to that in high heels. You stand in place and hop, kicking *both* heels in the back. The distance covered is unimportant. My son Kevin would use this final drill only when in top shape. Add this to your routine last.

Edmund R. Burke, Ph.D., an exercise physiologist who works with the U.S. Cycling Team, warns that like any

*(continued on page 78)*

## FLEXIBILITY DRILLS THAT BUILD SPEED

Here's a summary of drills designed to add flexibility and speed to your run. You should always warm up before (by jogging and stretching) and cool down after doing any such drills to avoid sore muscles. When starting a dynamic flexibility program, begin with only one or two drills, and gradually increase your capacity over a period of weeks and months. These drills are best done on your easy days, when you are running short and have more time to concentrate on nonspecific training activities.

They are best done during warm weather, when you also can utilize soft, smooth grass surfaces. Living in the Midwest, I consider flexibility drilling as more of a summer activity and weight lifting as more of a winter activity. Obviously, any training regimen in this or another book must be adapted to fit the realities of each runner's situation.

To do the drills, you need a straightaway 50 or 75 meters long, preferably grass or some soft surface. My son Kevin would do two to four repetitions of each of the drills, in the following order.

**1. High knees:** Probably the simplest drill, it is little more than running in place while moving forward gradually. Lift your knees high and land on the balls of your feet. Point your toes, with all movement straight ahead. The arms pump high in countermovement to the legs. Coach Sam Bell warns against doing high knees too fast, which may make it difficult to do the movements correctly.

**2. Fast feet:** Bill Bowerman described this as one means of teaching form to sprinters. This drill resembles high knees, except instead of emphasizing knee lift, you concentrate on moving your feet rapidly, almost pitter-patter. Straight-ahead movement with pointed toes is equally important here.

**3. High heels:** This exercise is easier than the two previous ones, and Kevin used it at this point partly to catch his breath. Runners new to flexibility drills probably should master this drill before attempting drills 4 and 5. It is simply running in place, like drill 1, but you kick your legs high in back instead of lifting your knees. Relax during this drill, and don't overemphasize speed.

**4. Skipping for height:** To skip, you must push off of one foot and land on that same (trail) foot before bringing your lead foot down. It is like the first two jumps of the triple jump. Skipping involves a pause, like the syncopated beat in music. In skipping for height (as with drill 1), emphasis is on high knee lift. During the pause, while suspended in midair, focus on getting your knee as high as possible.

**5. Skipping for distance:** This is the same as skipping for height, except the emphasis is on distance. Remember to keep all movement in a straight line. The two skipping drills require good flexibility, but they also promote flexibility. It could be said that drills 1, 2, and 3 help warm you up for drills 4 and 5.

**6. Bounding:** This is an elongated running action in which you concentrate on lifting your knees and striding with your arms up. It will become running unless you focus on knee lift. You also might compare this drill to the first jump of the triple jump: the hop.

**7. Double leg hop:** Not a drill for inexperienced runners. The movement is similar to that in drill 3, high heels. Stand in place and hop, kicking both heels in back. The distance covered is unimportant.

Once you master these speed-improvement drills and can do them without excessive fatigue or post-workout soreness, you can integrate them into different parts of your training week. Try them in the middle of your medium-distance workouts. I sometimes include several of the drills as part of my prerace warm-up (as described in chapter 4). High knees, high heels, and fast feet work well to loosen me up.

Also, don't ignore the stepping or standing variations of these drills. They may be more suitable for cold weather conditions or for those for whom too-vigorous drilling raises an unnecessary injury risk.

other type of training, bounding drills can lead to poor results if not used properly. "Symptoms of tendinitis and synovitis, particularly of the knee, can result from too much plyometric training," says Dr. Burke.

For distance runners, I don't recommend exercises that involve jumping on and off boxes and sideboards. Drills that promote dynamic flexibility—whether called bounding or plyometrics or ballistic stretching or learn-by-doing—do have their obvious place in the training program of a high school cross-country team. For one thing, the drills are sort of hokey. The kids enjoy doing them and can show off with the drills during their warm-ups. The well-trained athletes on college teams, such as those at Indiana and Oregon, also benefit by adding bounding to their program. But how appropriate are such drills for other runners, particularly those in the masters ranks? The risk of injury may be too great for many high-mileage runners, who are unused to speed drills and have limited flexibility.

Nevertheless, I believe that any runner can benefit by eventually adding at least some of the drills covered here to his or her training regimen. Benson's experience at his Florida Running Camp would suggest that this is so, since he has taught speed drills to many masters athletes who have attended his camps.

# Chapter 7

# SPEEDWORK

## FEEL THE DIFFERENCE BETWEEN FAST AND FAST

**T**here's only one way to get faster," Francie Larrieu Smith once told me. "You have to teach your legs what it feels like to run fast." She recommends some sort of speedwork, whether it be repeats, intervals, fartlek, or whatever. She concedes that runners can improve their times by slowly conditioning themselves—the same pace, day after day—but eventually, improvement ceases. Runners hit a plateau. That's when speedwork can help.

I need to get Larrieu Smith together with Allison Wolf, a member of the high school cross-country team I coach in Michigan City. Allison will be completing her senior year about the time this book is being published. She's captain of the team and a pretty good runner who runs in the mid–16-minute range for 4000 meters. Allison and I have a standing argument: I tell her she needs to do more speed-work, and in response, she tells me she doesn't have the speed for running speedwork.

It's an argument I hope to win the final summer before Allison's senior year. And if I win, she'll win, because Allie will improve to the point where she is capable of winning cross-country races at the dual meet level.

## THE RESULTS ARE WORTH THE EFFORT

A lot of runners are like Allison Wolf. They want to run fast, but they are unconvinced that they have either the ability or the determination to follow the advice of runners such as Larrieu Smith.

Once, at a meeting of our local running club, Joanne Kittel told me how much she despised speedwork. "Does it ever become fun?" she asked.

I had no ready answer. I find speedwork fun, maybe even exhilarating on occasion. Sure, I enjoy long runs through the woods or along backcountry roads—but there also are times when I want to get out on an ugly asphalt track and simply pound away. Is this being masochistic? Possibly so.

Talk to elite runners who average more than 100 miles a week in their training, and even they concede that quality is more important than quantity, that you can't abandon speedwork in favor of so-called junk miles. Very true.

During the club meeting, Kittel told me about the sort of speedwork she did. For one workout, she had marked a nearby road in 440-yard increments. Running over this marked road, she would alternate going fast and slow. It reminded me of some of the workouts of Emil Zatopek, who won the 5000, 10,000, and marathon in the 1952 Olympics. Zatopek would use telephone poles as guideposts for his sprints, sometimes also seeing how many poles he could reach while holding his breath. Such speedwork could hardly be classified as fun.

A second workout Kittel used was to go to a nearby golf course and do sprints of 130 yards, jogging and walking in between. I doubt if she knew much about Zatopek's training, but I recognized the source of inspiration for that second workout. It was my own method. I often described it at my clinics. Why did we both use 130 yards? Because that was the distance from one tree to another on a particularly flat fairway where I trained. Kittel even might have been using the same trees.

I enjoy that specific golf course workout, because I rarely push it. I go fast but seldom do so many repetitions that I finish tired. Typically, I do a set of eight sprints, jogging between, then walk to full recovery. When I am in top shape, I may do a second set of eight. I usually finish the workout feeling more refreshed than when I started. Why sets of eight? Why not? Good training is often as much an art as a science.

Does such a workout sound difficult or excessively painful to you? With those sprints done only slightly faster than race pace, and following a thorough warm-up, would they be likely to cause more injury than a long run on the road? Done in the cool early morning at sunrise in the bucolic setting of a golf course, would the workout lack beauty? I don't think so. And I believe that if you incorporate only this one workout into your training program for at least a few months during the summer, you will see an improvement in your running.

Like many fast runners, I came to road running with a track background: I competed in the mile in college and twice won a conference title in that event. To me, speedwork seems natural, but it could hardly seem so to Kittel, who, as I described in chapter 5, came to one of my running classes as your classic beginning jogger. Like most runners who are more involved with personal achievement than with Olympic aspirations, she began by running slow and progressed to running long. Speedwork, therefore, was unnatural to her. It was a beast to be conquered.

So it was not fun for Kittel. What was fun, however, was her 44:23 10-K finish several weeks before our conversation. It was her first 10-K under 45 minutes. And to what did she attribute the improvement?

Speedwork!

Kittel would continue to mix fast running with her long training, whether she liked it or not. Speedwork may not have been the only reason—or even the *major* reason—for her success. Over a period of years, she had built a base of miles that led to her improvement. But speedwork certainly contributed to her breaking 45 minutes for a 10-K.

# ARE YOU READY FOR THE CHALLENGE?

Before you begin to add speedwork to your training, you should consider whether you are yet ready to accept this discipline. Bob Glover of the New York Road Runners Club recommends that runners not use speed training until they train for one year, complete one race, run at least 15 miles per week, and race faster than their training pace at distances between 3 and 6 miles.

I might add to his list another recommendation: You should be willing to push into the discomfort zone. I dislike using the word *pain,* which has a negative connotation. I also find it difficult to understand why marathoners, who willingly suffer the agonies accompanying the last 6 miles of their race, are unwilling to accept what they consider to be painful sensations associated with speedwork. If you want to be a fast runner, you must be willing to accept a certain amount of discomfort. That doesn't mean speedwork is *all* discomfort. Integrated rest intervals act as a counterbalance. Just as quickly as you enter the discomfort zone, you leave it again by walking or jogging.

# WHY SPEED TRAINING WORKS

There are physiological reasons why speedwork is necessary if you want to maximize your potential at any distance, from the mile to the marathon. The primary reason, according to Ball State physiologist William Fink, is that you need to train your system to recruit the muscle fibers necessary to be able to run fast. "I must admit, a lot of the evidence is still out," suggests Fink, "but obtaining a sense of relaxation at race pace apparently comes as a result of training your muscle fibers to function at that accelerated pace."

But certain metabolic adaptations also occur, Fink explains, that relate to the pH levels of the muscles. When you run at an anaerobic level—that is, at a pace so fast you cannot absorb oxygen fast enough to eliminate the body's developing waste products—your muscles accumulate lactic acid. The pH level declines. Eventually, so much lactic acid accumulates in the muscles that they lose their ability to contract. This is why a middle-distance runner who sprints a 400-meter race usually crosses the line stiff-legged, in a state of near collapse. His muscles (at least temporarily) no longer function properly because of excessive lactic acid. Although the phenomenon occurs over a much longer period of time, the same happens to someone running a 5-K or 10-K.

Training, and particularly speed training, can modify this effect. According to Fink: "One of the adaptations is the development of a 'buffering' capacity on the part of the body. A runner who is well trained, through use of the proper amounts of speedwork, can limit the degree to which his muscles become acidic. He can run faster for a longer time before accumulation of lactic acid brings him to a halt."

Also part of the training process is the psychological ability to continue to perform under high stress: in effect, to push on through the pain barrier. But a lot of what many runners, including beginners, assume to be psychological adaptations may actually be metabolic ones—particularly pushing back the anaerobic threshold.

In the words of the late physiologist Dr. Al Claremont: "Too many people write themselves off as having bad bodies, when they possess more potential than they realize.

They simply are unwilling to do the hard work, including speed training, necessary to convert their supposed bad body into a good one."

The anaerobic threshold for someone with "poor" ability might be 50 percent of maximum; that is, they might begin to accumulate lactic acid in their muscles while running at half their maximum heart rate (MHR). For an "average" runner, it could be 70 percent, and a "good" runner may still be able to function aerobically at 85 percent of maximum. Speed-trained runners push into the world beyond. This level of conditioning permits runners like Gelindo Bordin to run seemingly endless miles below a 5-minute pace without apparent distress, because lactic acid has not yet started to accumulate. But even a less-gifted runner can push his anaerobic threshold to the right of the scale: from 50 percent toward 85 percent. And the way to do this, as Joanne Kittel discovered and, hopefully, as Allison Wolf *will* discover, is by doing speedwork.

Not all of us are born physiologically equal, and it is true—despite my running argument with Allison—that some possess more speed than others. Ball State's Dr. David Costill popularized the theory of fast-twitch vs. slow-twitch muscles. As I mentioned in chapter 2, everybody is blessed with both. Most of us have equal numbers of each, but some have more of one than the other. Along with biomechanical differences, this is one reason why some people succeed as sprinters, and others, as distance runners.

Fast-twitch muscles fire quickly, of course, but also quickly exhaust their supply of fuel in the form of glycogen. They are good for short bursts of energy. Slow-twitch muscles contract more slowly, but they maintain that contraction for a longer period of time. They are good for activities that require continuous effort.

Along with these two basic types, scientists recognize a third type of muscle that fits somewhere in the middle: a fast-twitch muscle that can be trained for endurance, or a slow-twitch muscle that can be trained for speed. In an article in *Esquire* on the subject, Kevin Shyne wrote: "Although it's long been believed that the ratio of fast- to slow-twitch fibers is genetically determined, a number of coaches and sports scientists have recently challenged that view. They hold that speed is much more learnable than previously believed and that anyone can substantially improve his or ability to run fast through proper training."

Bob Glover states: "Many runners, especially beginning racers, underestimate their abilities as athletes. Through speed training, they often discover that they are tougher than they had realized."

Apart from physiological considerations, I look upon speedwork as a fine-tuning device, a means by which you become able to extract the maximum amount of energy from an already well-conditioned machine, the human body. Speedwork is a training method that may allow you, after many months or even years of long, steady running, to continue to progress after you seem to have reached a performance plateau.

Speed also is important for tactical reasons. The University of Oregon's Bill Dellinger says: "The distance runner who has the potential to sprint at the end of a race has a distinct advantage. He can relax and allow the other runners to do all the pacing, relying on his ability to accelerate at the finish. It's known as a kick.

"The problem," he adds, "is that distance runners spend hundreds of hours and thousands of miles training, yet neglect that one weapon—acceleration, or the ability to sprint—that all would love to have."

# FINDING YOUR
# SPEEDWORK PACE

What is speedwork? Speedwork consists of any training done at race pace or faster. This definition allows for variation in abilities. But by what "race" do you define race pace? During the course of a year, I may compete at distances from 800 meters to a marathon, and while my range is greater than that of many competitive runners, it is not untypical.

Frank Shorter relates race pace to his average speed in a 2-mile run. During the period when he ranked as one of the world's top 10,000-meter runners, Shorter would consider speedwork as running done faster than 65 seconds for a 400. I relate more to the 5-K to 10-K. A number of respected coaches, from Dr. Jack Daniels to Bob Glover to Dr. Owen Anderson, who write for *Runner's World* and other publications, tie speedwork to the 10-K because it's the most popular race distance and most runners can easily relate to it. Since my most recent 10-K times have been in the 36-minute range, my speedwork begins around 90 seconds for a 400.

Choose your pace carefully. A common beginner's mistake is to run the speedwork flat out—beyond race pace. If Joanne Kittel related speedwork to her 10-K best, 44:23, her benchmark would be around 2 minutes for each 440-yard increment she marked for her workout. Allison Wolf would fit somewhere between Kittel's and my paces. It is all based on individual abilities.

# *SPEEDWORK COMES IN MANY VARIETIES*

There are various forms of speedwork: some of them quite difficult, some of them quite easy, some of them quite similar, some of them quite different. Different coaches have favored certain forms over others, based partly on their own intuitive perception of what works best for their athletes. And a form of speedwork that works best for one athlete may not necessarily work best for others.

Some forms of speedwork are best for improving strength, others, for improving endurance. Some help you with your form, others, with your concentration. Another important consideration is the confidence that comes from training hard in a measured environment. How you do your speedwork may depend on your specific situation and surroundings. Your training plans will be dictated by whether you live near a track, a golf course, or a wooded area with trails, for example. Weather conditions may be a factor, as will be the length and importance of the race for which you're training.

In this chapter, I'll cover one type of speedwork, called repeats. In the chapters ahead, I'll also describe intervals, sprints, strides, surges, fartlek, and hill training—and how to successfully implement and use them in your training schedule.

# *REPEATS*

A repeat workout is one in which you run very fast, usually over a very short distance, and take a relatively long period of time to recover before repeating that distance again.

A typical repeat workout for me might be 3 × 300 meters. I run 300 meters flat out and walk until fully recovered (usually one lap around the track, about 5 minutes). I *repeat* the 300 two more times.

Running repeats was the first type of training I encountered when I went out for track as a youngster. It was a simple, basic method for working on your speed, one employed by sprinters as well as distance runners.

Repeat running, as taught by many track coaches, was a fairly unsophisticated form of training. It was easy for a coach to pull out a stopwatch and tell his runners to sprint a fast lap. After timing the runners, he could tell them to "walk it off" while he gave his attention to the high-jumpers or shot-putters. Looking up 5 minutes later, he would see his runners standing around and send them sprinting around the track again.

At a luncheon in New York sponsored by *The Runner*, Glenn Cunningham, America's greatest miler in the 1930s, described to me the training methods that had brought him close to 4 minutes for that distance. Cunningham ran repeats, claiming he rarely ran more than a dozen miles a week. All the milers from that era trained similarly.

I graduated from college in 1953 and, during graduate school, trained with Ted Haydon at the University of Chicago. Haydon patterned his training after that of Billy Hayes, the successful Indiana University coach whose runners included Don Lash and Fred Wilt. After an overdistance run of 3 miles on Mondays, we would do three or four 440s on Tuesdays, a couple of 880s on Wednesdays, five or six 220s on Thursdays, rest on Fridays, and race 2 miles on Saturdays, taking Sundays off. Although it was not identified as such, our training consisted mostly of repeats, because we paid little attention to what we did between fast runs. We recovered by jogging, walking, or sometimes, sitting down.

In 1956, I traveled to Berlin to participate as a member of a U.S. team in the Conseil Internationale du Sport Militaire (CISM) Championships, a track-and-field meet for athletes serving in the armed forces of various nations. On the team was Tom Courtney, a Fordham University graduate who would win the 800 meters at the Olympic Games later that year, running 1:47.7. He also had won the National AAU 400 title that same year.

I would like to tell you that I trained with Courtney, but as someone with considerably less speed, I mostly watched as he ran through a series of 300-meter repeats. Courtney explained that he would begin the track season running 8 × 300; then as he got fitter and faster, he would cut the number and the time. At peak training, he would run 3 × 300 at full speed.

It seemed like a reasonable way to train, so eventually I copied Courtney's workout, modifying it to my own needs as a distance runner. I developed a pattern for repeat running, which I described as "three of something." Three became my magic number. I rarely did more, because too many repetitions converted a speed workout into an endurance workout. My body quickly told me that to do more than three, I would need to slow down. The purpose of the workout was to run near maximum speed. There was nothing scientific about my approach. It simply felt right.

Typical workouts that I still use when coaching high school runners are 3 × 200, 3 × 300, and 3 × 400, or for variation, a 200, a 300, and a 400. I seldom go beyond one lap on a track anymore, although years ago, one of my favorite workouts was to crowd 3 flat-out miles within the space of an hour. Were I to do that workout today, it would probably be over a measured road course. At peak training, I include one repeat workout in my schedule each week—but never exactly the same workout. For psychological reasons, I do not want to be able to look at this week's workout and realize that I ran ¹/₁₀ second slower than last week.

Dr. Anderson recommends that each rest period be about five times as long as it takes you to run each fast repeat. Such a 1 to 5 ratio sounds about right to me. Usually I would rest by walking the same distance that I had just run. After finishing a 300, I would turn and walk back to where I had started. If I felt I needed more time to recover after I arrived back at the starting line, I would take it. With several of my high school runners, I sometimes found that they liked to jog and walk back to the start, anxious to go again. I'd hold them to a 5-minute break to make certain they were well rested. I would watch them and talk to them, and if they looked like they needed more time, I would give them more time. I stressed to them, and I stress to you, that repeats should *not* be a punishing workout. You should finish a repeat workout refreshed, feeling positive about running hard with good form.

## CONTROL THE INTENSITY FOR BEST RESULTS

One word of caution (I mentioned it before, but I think it's important enough to repeat): Runners new to speedwork (particularly masters runners) should not begin by running repeats flat out. Build your speedwork the way you build your distance. Start easy and gradually increase the intensity. A good beginning speed for repeats is your race pace for the full length of the repeat. Over a period of weeks and months, improve your total time by gradually accelerating toward the end of each repeat. Try to maintain enough control so you can finish each repeat at a speed faster than you start.

In training runners in Dallas, coach Robert Vaughan has them run 400s with the second 200 faster than the first. If you finish your repeats struggling and with your form deteriorating, you're running too far, too fast, or too many. Pick a distance, speed, and number that you can run while maintaining good speed form.

That's one reason why I like 300 meters as a distance for repeats. It's longer than the sprint distances of 100 and 200 meters, so you don't (or shouldn't) run it full speed. And it's shorter than 400 meters, so you stop before lactic acid slows your pace and tightens your legs.

On most tracks, the start for the 300 meters is after the first turn, at the beginning of the back straightaway. That's also the starting line for the 1500 meters. In instructing my runners, I recommend that they begin relatively slowly in the first 100 meters down the back straightaway, build through the second 100 meters coming around the turn, and then kick the final 100 meters down the home straightaway. I ask them to visualize running the last 300 meters of their races. Repeats thus become an exercise to fine-tune a finishing kick. When the runners reach that point in a race, they can relate their kick to the repeats they run in practice.

At Indiana University, track coach Sam Bell uses a similar philosophy, but he fine-tunes his runners using 150-meter sprints. Bell has had a series of fine milers on his teams, and he feels that the last turn and final straightaway of a 1500 is where the race is won or lost. But regardless of the distance you choose for repeats, they should be done with control.

In an article translated from Russian and published in *Track Technique,* Soviet coach A. Yakimov advises: "Repetition training is not a sprint nor a run at full strength. The athlete runs at a set and controlled pace, which depends on what distance and pace he is preparing himself for. This type of training is a method for developing speed and speed endurance, and can be considered as a method used to develop tempo and a sense of pace. Repetition training brings out a reaction from the body similar to that of a race. So this method finds its main use in the competitive season."

## USE REST INTERVALS WISELY

"Some runners rest sitting down," Yakimov states. "At this they have noticed that the heart rate drops to normal faster than when jogging. However, the recovery of the heart rate is not the only important issue. It's possible that it's better to jog than sit, especially after an intense run. Slow running offers the muscles a massaging effect, which helps clear waste products and increase the supply to the muscles of oxygen and sugar. In repetition work, the rest should consist of jogging followed by walking, and then sitting or lying down."

When doing repeat miles on the track while at the University of Chicago, I'd walk or jog over to the gymnasium and lie down on the wrestling mats during my 20-minute recovery period. This had the advantage of getting me out of the heat and the sun, since I usually did this workout in midsummer. Today, while doing repeat 400s, I sometimes will continue around the track, walking 100 meters, jogging 200 meters down the back straightaway and around the turn, then walking 100 meters down the home straightaway before running hard again.

Why? Because it feels right. Every runner needs to determine the best form of rest for his or her particular needs.

Yakimov notes that lengthening the rest intervals (within certain limits) and going faster on the runs increases the workout's effect on speed. Conversely, shortening the rest periods and slowing the runs decreases the effect on speed and increases the influence on endurance.

He offered the table on page 92 for determining how long to rest during various forms of speed training. You also can use this table for interval training (see chapter 8).

Yakimov failed to include my favorite distance, 300 meters, in his table. Had he done so, his rest period would probably have come close to matching the 5-minute rest I suggest. When I ran 3 × 1 mile, my rest periods probably were close to the 20 minutes the Soviet coach recommends

## Yakimov's Table of Rest Intervals

| Distance of Fast Run (in meters) | Length of Rest (in minutes) | | |
|---|---|---|---|
| | Easy Pace | Hard Pace | Flat-Out Pace |
| 100 | up to 0:30 | up to 1:30 | up to 3:00 |
| 200 | 1:00 | 2:00 | 4:00 |
| 400 | 1:30 | 3:00 | 7:00 |
| 800 | 2:30 | 5:00 | 9:00 |
| 1000 | 3:00 | 6:00 | 12:00 |
| 1200 | 4:00 | 7:00 | 15:00 |
| 2000 | 5:00 | 8:00 | 20:00 |

for runners doing 2000-meter repeats, ¼ mile longer. What many coaches determine scientifically, runners learn intuitively. Actually, the best coaches simply watch the workouts done by intuitive runners, learn from them, and systematize their training for the benefit of other runners.

## SHARPEN YOUR RUNNING ECONOMY

Repeats also promote running economy. Writing in *Runner's World,* Dr. Anderson describes research by a team of exercise scientists from Arizona State University that followed miler Steve Scott's training over a period of nine months during 1980 and 1981.

Scott improved his running economy by 5 percent, but, Dr. Anderson suggests, only after he added fast 200- to 600-meter runs to his training program. After improving his economy, Scott set two American records: 3:31.96 for 1500 meters and 3:49.68 for the mile.

Dr. Anderson advises: "The key to improving economy is to run fast while you're feeling strong and relaxed, not when you're tired and struggling and your running style is unnatural and fatigued."

# Chapter 8

# INTERVAL TRAINING

## A POWERFUL TOOL TO IMPROVE SPEED

**T**om Ecker, an expert on coaching techniques from Iowa, once described interval training as "the most effective single training system ever devised." Ball State's Dr. David Costill claims that a runner shifting to interval training often can improve speed after only a single session. The University of Oregon's Bill Dellinger states: "Interval training—if it's done properly—develops speed in a runner more quickly than any other form of training."

The magic workout? If I had to name one single type of training capable of converting a plodder into a runner, this would be it. Interval training, carefully structured into a well-designed workout regimen, may not necessarily turn you into an Olympian, but it can make you a better runner.

An article by Brian Mitchell in *Athletics Weekly* presented the case for interval training: "In this type of [training], the runner gets the best of two worlds, because he keeps moving throughout and is able regularly to raise the pace above what would be done in a steady run, and thereby also extend the range of body movement, with all that implies for muscles and nerves. The session is under as much control as you want. It is systematic and definite, and it is tailored for each individual, so long as he does not allow himself to be overrun by a group of fellow athletes and forced to go their pace rather than his own."

Mitchell adds: "Interval training can also be intelligently progressive, month by month, season by season, accessible and adjustable."

If proof were needed of the effectiveness of interval training, James Stray-Gundersen, M.D., provided it during a study he did in collaboration with Peter Snell at the University of Texas in Dallas. The researchers asked ten experienced runners, whose 10-K times averaged between 34 and 42 minutes, to train six weeks at 50 miles a week, building a base. They then divided the runners: One group did lactate threshold training, the other group did interval work—400s in 75 to 85 seconds, 200s in 33 to 38 seconds.

At the end of ten weeks of training, the researchers tested both groups by having them race at 800- and 10,000-meter distances. Preliminary analysis showed that the interval-trained group improved their 800 times by 11.2 seconds and their 10,000 times by more than 2 minutes. The control group demonstrated lesser improvements: 6.6 seconds in the 800 and just over 1 minute in the 10,000. Improvements in $VO_2$ max showed a similar division: 12 percent in the interval group, 4 percent in the control group.

Dr. Stray-Gundersen and Snell worked with well-conditioned runners. But at the University of Miami, Arlette C. Perry, Ph.D., tested 66 college-age women in an aerobic dance class, training two groups three days a week for 35 minutes a day at 75 to 85 percent of their maximum heart rate (MHR). The control group did aerobics 35 minutes nonstop. The interval group alternated 3 to 5 minutes of aerobics with brisk walking, stretching the workout past

35 minutes. After 12 weeks, the control group had improved cardiovascular endurance by 8 percent; the interval group had improved by 18 percent.

Liz Kauffman, writing in *American Health,* described a similar study at the University of Massachusetts involving subjects training on stationary bicycles. Two groups of cyclists covered the same distance in 12-minute exercise sessions, three days weekly. One group rode steadily; an interval group alternated between hard and easy paces. At the end of 12 weeks, the steady-rate group had not improved fitness; the interval group had improved by 11 percent.

At Arizona State University, Douglas L. Conley, Ed.D., trained one distance runner for 18 weeks, beginning with 30 miles a week and increasing distance gradually over a period of ten weeks. As fitness improved, the number of interval sessions was increased from one a week to four a week.

In the first ten weeks, the runner's $VO_2$ max improved from an already high 69.1 to 71.6. With the introduction of interval training, his $VO_2$ max jumped within the next five weeks to a sky-high 77.6. Dr. Conley deduced that interval training played a much greater role than endurance training in the elevation of $VO_2$ max and suspected, as he wrote in *The Physician and Sportsmedicine,* that its major contribution "is the promotion of economical running at the pace demands of competition." In his article, he also quoted Dr. Costill as saying that repeated bouts of speedwork stimulate the recruitment of muscle fibers and simulate patterns of movement to be used during competition.

All research studies suggest that regardless of your sport or level of condition, you can make significant improvement in your fitness level by using some form of interval training. Let's discuss this magic training method in greater detail.

# WHAT IS INTERVAL TRAINING?

"Contrary to popular belief," says coach Dellinger, "interval training isn't superfast, all-out running as much as it is controlled running." Control, of course, is important in any intelligent training program. The subtle difference between running repeats (as covered in chapter 7) and doing interval training—other than the fact that you usually include more repetitions in the latter—is that you control the rest interval *between* the fast runs as well as the speed and distance you are running.

That's an important point. The key word is *between*. Many runners mistakenly refer to intervals as the fast part of the speedwork. Not so. The word *interval* is literally defined as an intervening period of time, a period of temporary cessation, or a pause.

Remember that. The interval is the rest that happens between. The fast run is more properly referred to as the *repetition* (although this term can be confused with repeats). Many coaches call the fast segments "reps."

But what's more important than what you call them is how you do them.

## A METHOD PERFECTED IN GERMANY

The individual credited with the development of interval training as an important means of improving speed and endurance is the German coach Waldermar Gerschler, whose prime pupil was former world record holder Rudolf Harbig. In 1939, Harbig ran a 1:46.6 for 800 meters, a mark that remained on the books for nearly two decades, long after he was killed in World War II.

Gerschler was not the first coach to ask his athletes to alternate fast and slow running. Earlier, the Finnish coach Pehhala had developed a system of "terrace training," which consisted of repeated speed runs with slower running between. Czechoslovakia's Emil Zatopek also employed this pattern in his training, running as much as 60 × 400, although slower than race pace. After Zatopek's three victories at the 1952 Olympics, coaches and athletes began to examine his training methods. They realized the advantages of fast/slow training: Most important, runners could work at race paces for race distances and with race intensities by utilizing recovery segments at midworkout.

Gerschler's contribution was to systemize interval training, which he did in collaboration with Hans Reindell, M.D., a cardiologist. Reportedly, Gerschler and Dr. Reindell studied more than 3,000 individuals. According to an article by Paul A. Smith in *Athletics Journal*, the German coach and physician together pinpointed when the greatest stimulus for heart development occurs—during the first 10 seconds of the recovery interval. "The run provides the stress, while the interval allows for the development response," Smith explained. "Because Gerschler and Reindell realized during their research that the rest period was the key to development, they named this exercise 'interval' training." And it became a successful formula for improving speed and endurance that could be applied to almost any workout, at any level.

Before going any further, I should note that there was little (or no) "masters" competition when Gerschler and Dr. Reindell did their research. So we can assume they worked with young athletes, whose MHRs would have been around 200. If so, heart rates around 170 to 180 beats a minute for the fast run would have been the equivalent of 85 to 90 percent of their MHRs. Heart rates of 130 to 140 beats a minute during the recovery would have been the equivalent of 65 to 70 percent of their MHRs.

## FIVE SIMPLE COMPONENTS OF A POWERFUL ROUTINE

In describing interval training, Gerschler and Dr. Reindell identified the following five variables.

**1. Distance:** How far you run during each repetition. Gerschler and Dr. Reindell determined that the time for each run should not exceed 90 seconds. (This suggested a distance no longer than 600 meters, although 400 meters became the distance most favored by runners for interval workouts.) The intensity should be sufficient to produce a heart rate of 170 to 180 beats per minute, which they measured during the first 10 seconds of the recovery period.

**2. Interval:** How long you rest during each interval. They also deduced that the interval should not exceed 90 seconds. They noted that it took only 30 seconds into the interval for the pulse to drop to approximately 130 beats per minute. If the pulse failed to fall below 140, they slowed the pace or shortened the distance. If the pulse remained elevated, they stopped the workout.

**3. Repetitions:** How many times you run the distance.

**4. Pace:** How fast you run the specified distance.

**5. Rest:** What you do during the interval.

Let me offer you an example based on my own training. While researching this book, I visited the National Institute for Fitness and Sport in Indianapolis to interview Dean Brittenham. It was December, and I arrived early to use the institute's indoor track: 200 meters, approximately eight laps to the mile. The institute is located a short distance from the Indiana University and Purdue University in Indianapolis (I.U.P.U.I.) outdoor track used for the 1984 and 1988 Olympic Trials.

For various reasons, I decided that morning to run 300-meter repetitions, a lap and a half on the track. Thus, that became my *distance,* the first variable. The distance usually remains constant during any single workout, but may vary from one workout to the next. "The important thing," says Ecker, "is that the distance is shorter than the athlete's race distance, usually in multiples of 100."

At the institute, fast runners are asked to use the outside lanes, leaving the inside lanes for walkers and joggers. I chose lane 5, which meant that after finishing each 300, I would need to continue around the track approximately another 140 meters to get back to the starting line. This became my *interval,* the second variable.

Not knowing how I would feel, since this was my first run on the institute's track, I simply ran until I felt I had a good workout. I stopped after 11 *repetitions,* the third variable. "The exact number of runs is not important," says Ecker. "The important thing is that they have run to their absolute limit." Ecker considers this the biggest guessing game the coach (or athlete) has to play. "If too low, [the number of reps] reduces the effectiveness of the workout," he says. "If too high, the runner crashes."

My time for each 300 varied, around 61 or 62 seconds—although borrowing a tip from coach Dellinger, I ran two of my reps (the 6th and the 11th) faster, 58 and 56 seconds. (More on Dellinger's theories later.) The *pace* I ran was the fourth variable. "The speed of each repeat run," suggests Ecker, "is determined by the runner's projected race pace."

Between reps, I jogged at a moderate speed, covering the 140-meter interval distance in 60 to 65 seconds. (That converts to approximately 12-minute miles, 5 mph.)

The *rest* between bouts of running fast was the fifth and final variable. "For interval training to be a truly effective system for conditioning the runner's cardiorespiratory system," says Ecker, "the heart rate must be alternately increased during the runs and decreased to a level of semirecovery between runs."

This resulted in a rather neat workout package: 1 minute of hard running followed by 1 minute of easy running, repeated 11 times. My heart rate on the fast runs rose to above 90 percent of my MHR; during the intervals, it dropped to 70 percent of my MHR.

Gerschler would have been proud of me, had he been present to witness the workout. As a German scientist, he also would have been fascinated with the digital watch I wore (capable of storing 30 times) that allowed me to precisely record the times for my reps and intervals. The fact that I was wearing a second watch that recorded my pulse every 5 seconds would have convinced Gerschler that indeed, he had been born in the wrong era.

The record of that particular workout appears on page 100. Keep in mind that my maximum heart rate is 150, or slightly higher.

In shortened form, the workout could be described as: 11 × 300 (61.1 seconds average), 140 rest between (65.1 seconds average). That sounds scientific, but actually I just showed up at the track and did what my body told me was a reasonable workout for my level of training and my feelings of energy on that particular morning. I might add that I finished the workout comfortably, feeling that I put in some hard work that felt good, whether or not it would help me in my next race.

## An Interval Workout

| Number | Rep Time (in seconds) | Pulse Rate (in beats per minute) | Interval Time (in seconds) | Pulse Rate (in beats per minute) |
|---|---|---|---|---|
| 1 | 62.1 | 136 | 63.5 | 103 |
| 2 | 61.0 | 138 | 63.4 | 108 |
| 3 | 61.4 | 141 | 65.9 | 105 |
| 4 | 61.5 | 140 | 65.4 | 106 |
| 5 | 61.2 | 142 | 65.1 | 109 |
| 6 | 58.7 | 147 | 65.9 | 109 |
| 7 | 64.0 | 140 | 60.1 | 109 |
| 8 | 63.3 | 141 | 62.3 | 111 |
| 9 | 61.3 | 145 | 65.4 | 111 |
| 10 | 61.6 | 144 | 66.7 | 110 |
| 11 | 56.2 | 150 | 72.6 | 111 |

That single well-measured workout would provide a data base for future workouts. One week later, I was in New York City on business and worked out one morning on the cinder path (approximately 2000 meters around) that circles the reservoir in Central Park. I set my watch to beep every 60 seconds to remind me to alternate running fast and slow. I ran 11 fast sprints in this manner, jogging between. My measured heart rates were slightly lower than in Indianapolis, possibly because chilly weather prevented me from going full tilt. Otherwise, this New York workout was a carbon copy of the first. While interval training most often is done on the track, it need not be.

# WHY DO INTERVAL TRAINING?

Interval running, even at relatively slow speeds, is more demanding than ordinary running. It is a high-stress workout. It also can be more time-consuming. You may need to travel to a track, or somewhere flat and marked, to do it.

Many runners ask, why train that hard when jogging in the park is more fun and less stressful?

The main reason for interval training, of course, is improvement. Although some may consider interval training painful, it actually can be a rather benign way to train at race pace. Certainly, running 400 meters at your best pace for 10,000 meters, then slowing down to rest before doing another, is easier than running 25 laps at your best pace. Practically all research done on distance runners suggests that they improve when they add intensity to their programs. The other side of that coin, of course, is a study of walkers and joggers by Michael L. Pollock, Ph.D., director of the University of Florida's Center for Exercise Science, that shows that intensity is exactly what scares beginners away. It also gets them injured more, says Dr. Pollock, and I'll buy that. As a result, when you mention intensity, or interval training, to the people who run for T-shirts in 10-K races, they get Little Orphan Annie eyes. Their eyeballs go blank. They don't want to go fast or do speedwork; they just want to get in their daily 5 miles and burn a few calories to feel good and look good.

If that is your approach, please don't change. Yet beyond a desire to improve race times, those who embrace intensity comprehend that there is a mystical aspect to interval training. Wringing yourself dry *can* be exhilarating. Interval training done in the company of like-minded fellow runners results in a shared experience, even if you're too stressed during or afterward to talk. Being able to see improvement from week to week also offers a form of motivation. And interval training can improve your concentration and refine your technique and form.

# MORE ART THAN SCIENCE

How fast should you do your interval training? That's a tricky question, despite all the expert advice and the charts published in running magazines that seem to offer exact answers. A good coach observing you in training over a period of six months or more might be able to tell you how fast to run—or he might not. Coaching remains somewhat of a guessing game. It's more art than science. People differ in their abilities, and they also differ in their ability to train hard on the track. Someone new to interval training certainly would find it more stressful than an old hand like myself.

Jim Huff, a coach who works with members of the Motor City Striders in Detroit, warns against setting too-precise goals for interval workouts. "Runners get frustrated if you say run a certain speed and they can't accomplish that, so any time set has to be realistic," he explains. "You can't just read what other people do and try to copy their workouts."

Dr. Owen Anderson suggests in *Running Research News* that interval training be carried out at an intensity of 90 to 100 percent of your MHR—about the same intensity as a 10-K race. Thus, a good starting point for most people beginning interval training is to train at a slightly faster pace than you run in a 10-K race, or at about the same pace you might run a 5-K. Some coaches also suggest that if your racing goal is a 5-K, then you should train at your speed for the mile, or 1500 meters. Milers should train at half-mile pace, and so forth.

Peter Snell advises against running interval 400s at faster than race pace. He told Dr. Anderson: "It is tempting to run fast during your workouts, but remember that you're not going to be able to run that fast in a race. If you run too fast during workouts, you'll get too fatigued to do good training, and you'll also get out of your race rhythm. Too much speed is more damaging than too much distance."

Training at race pace does have another important advantage. You develop pace judgment. During the interval phase of my running career, I could almost tell how fast I had run each quarter without looking at my watch or waiting for the coach beside the track to call my time. On occasion, I've participated in "prediction miles," where the winner is not the fastest runner but rather the one able to predict his or her time. The enviable purpose, of course, is to allow less-experienced runners to win a few trophies in an event where speed is not a factor. Inevitably, the fastest runners still win, because they are most likely to have honed their pace judgment through interval training. In one prediction mile, I embarrassed myself and got all the other contestants upset with me by selecting a time somewhere around 9 minutes, finishing well behind almost everybody who entered, yet still winning because I nailed my time within a few seconds.

My ability to tell you exactly the pace I'm running has recently faded somewhat, because I more often do even my interval training away from the track. But I still possess a well-developed ability to sense pace changes of even a few seconds per mile by others running around me in races. This is an important skill, because running at a consistent speed is one way to conserve energy.

# *SETTING REALISTIC GOALS*

At the University of Oregon, Bill Dellinger utilizes a system of interval training, borrowed from his predecessor Bill Bowerman, that revolves around *date pace* and *goal pace.* Date pace is the pace at which you can currently run your race distance. Goal pace is the pace at which you hope to run that distance toward the end of the season—that is, in the important meets. For top University of Oregon athletes, that meet is the NCAA championships. For me, it's the World Veterans Championships, where I plan to run the 5000 meters, or possibly the 2000-meter steeplechase. To fine-tune my speed for those distances, I would also do several 1500-meter races leading up to that meet. So in doing interval training, I need to work at paces I would be running in races between 1500 and 5000 meters.

When I threw those two fast 300s into the middle of the workout in Indianapolis, which I mentioned earlier, I actually was following a variation of the Oregon interval system. I was running the reps at a pace near what I felt I could accomplish at that time. A 300-meter pace of 61.1 maintained for 1500 meters would give me a final time of 5:05.6 for that distance. However, if I could maintain the

58.7 I ran in my sixth quarter, or the 56.2 I ran in my final quarter, I could run 4:53.5 or 4:41.0, respectively.

I was far from being in peak shape during that midwinter workout in Indianapolis, but I had run 4:53.3 the previous August at the 1990 TAC Masters Track-and-Field Championships in the same city. And at the 1989 TAC meet in San Diego, I had run 4:45.9, placing third. For 1991, I was setting my pace higher, so that day's training in Indianapolis seemed quite compatible with my plan. I should mention again that I did not set out that morning to run date pace and goal pace. I simply got out on the track and ran, allowing my body to tell me my level. I was able to do that because of the experience from decades of interval training.

Less-experienced runners need to set their date and race paces for interval workouts carefully. Bowerman believed that runners should feel exhilarated, not exhausted, at the end of a workout. "Too many individuals," he said, "simply run themselves into the ground and aren't fresh enough to race properly." He felt that if runners overwork, they become less excited about racing.

That's assuming that racing is the most important reason that you run. For the college coach, the race—whether during cross-country season or part of a track meet—certainly is *the* reason, the *raison d'être* of running. This was particularly true for Bowerman in 1972, the year he served as head track-and-field coach for the U.S. Olympic team. If your end goal is developing Olympic champions, then certainly interval training provides a very effective means to that end.

But 1972 was the year that Frank Shorter won the Olympic marathon. Frank's victory was not the only reason for the running boom that followed soon after, but ironically, it played an important part in forcing an expansion of the goals available to runners. Not every runner has Shorter's talent, or even a fraction of that talent. Not every runner is training for an Olympic medal. Life for most runners today is more than an endless quest for one more race T-shirt or trophy. Most of today's runners don't even race, or when they do, they run races more for social reasons than for success. We've redefined our goals since the time that Bowerman was coaching at Oregon, so that the means often may be more important than the end. The workout is more important than the race. Ironically, Bowerman was one of the early pioneers in the fitness movement, teaching jogging to housewives as an aside to training elite athletes.

Perhaps I reflect my own philosophy, because I find myself able to secure as much masochistic enjoyment from a single well-crafted workout—a hard run in the park, a set of quarters strung together on the track—as from winning my age-group in a megarace. I still measure myself in megaraces, but hard running carries its own rewards. Interval training, because of the way it can be measured in bits and pieces, can provide a form of satisfaction akin to racing. That is not to say that Bowerman and other dedicated coaches are wrong for their emphasis on racing as the end product. There is room within running for many philosophies. You don't need to race to run fast.

Nevertheless, there is nothing like competition to provide a level of motivation not experienced in practice. In describing a downhill ski race on television, Curry Chapman, retired coach of the Canadian women's national team, suggested that the viewer should think of a string tied at the starting line and leading through the gates to the finish line. "In training," Chapman said, "there's slack in the string. Race day, adrenalin pulls the string tighter."

# *MOVING ON TO REACHING YOUR PEAK*

Therefore, races provide a goal that can be approached with logical and systematic training. Interval training, of course, lends itself extremely well to progressive programs, ones in which you begin at a relatively low level of fitness and train progressively harder to improve performance. You go from weakness to strength via the overload principle. This can be accomplished in several ways.

Writing in *Athletics Journal*, Donald E. Boggis, Jr., a

high school coach from Hollis, New Hampshire, discussed manipulation of the five variables in progressively overloading (and strengthening) the system. Boggis cited variables slightly different from those mentioned by coach Gerschler and others, but the effect is the same. As your training program progresses, suggests Boggis, you can increase the number of repetitions, or you can increase the speed you run them. You can decrease the amount of rest you take during the interval by jogging farther, or you can increase the distance of the repetitions, maintaining the same pace. An infinite number of combinations present themselves.

Yet blind application of any number-based system can cause problems. Fatigue, poor diet, and lack of sleep all can affect the intensity of your training. An additional variable—one not mentioned in most coaching articles—is weather. Cold, heat, wind, and rain can affect how fast or how far you run during any given workout.

Nevertheless, the advantage of training using an overload program is that it does provide a strong psychological carrot as you peak for a specific race. It's like runners in training for a marathon, who progressively increase the length of their weekend runs to where they finally can cover 20 miles comfortably the last month before they are asked to race 26. It's like the countdown before the launch of a space shuttle. After the long runs to develop endurance, after the fast runs to develop strength, you use a shot of speed training featuring intervals to fine-tune your speed. Because it lends itself to progressive manipulation (as suggested by Boggis), interval training offers an effective way of peaking.

Maintaining that peak is another matter. In discussing the benefits of interval training, Gerschler and Dr. Reindell commented: "Interval training saves time, is a good stimulant, but its disadvantage is that the achieved condition is not maintained for a long period."

Magic workout, no—but if you expect to run fast, you probably need to include some form of interval training in your regular regimen.

# *INNOVATIONS THAT MAKE CHAMPIONS*

I first discovered the advantages of interval training while living in Germany in the mid-1950s. Gerschler was still training runners in that country at that time, but our paths never crossed. I knew him only by reputation.

I was a member of the United States Army, stationed in Germany from May 1955 to November 1956. I ran every day, not always with the Army's permission. While a member of the 63rd Tank Battalion in Kitzingen, I sometimes would crawl under a barbed wire fence at the end of the day to run in a nearby forest. Later, while working as an ordinance draftsman at Seventh Army Headquarters in Vaihingen, outside Stuttgart, I would appear at the camp exit at 9:00 at night dressed in running gear. The guards at the gate probably thought I was crazy, but they waved me through when I showed them my pass. I remember those runs through what was truly the Schwarzwald ("dark forest") as among the most enjoyable workouts of my career.

On other occasions, usually on weekends, I would drive into town to train on the track of the VfB Stuttgart, a local sports club. Accompanying me was another soldier stationed at the post: Dean Thackwray, who made the 1956 U.S. Olympic team in the marathon. Our frequent training partner was Stefan Lupfert, who won several German indoor championships at 3000 meters and also competed on the national team in the 3000-meter steeplechase.

Dissatisfied with my previous training methods, I already had begun to increase the number of repetitions. But while training with Lupfert, I saw how he ran somewhat slower reps but jogged much faster between those reps, typically at about an 8-minute-mile pace. A standard workout for us back then was 12 × 400, with a 400 jog between. The fast 400s were done in around 65 or 70 seconds, the slow 400s (or intervals) in 2 minutes.

Also in Germany at that time was Frank McBride, whom I had run against in college when he competed for South

Dakota State. McBride placed seventh in the 1500 meters at the 1952 U.S. Olympic Trials, and he later achieved success as a masters runner. But at this period in his life, McBride was serving as a coach of Army runners stationed in Germany, first as an officer, later as a Department of the Army civilian. McBride was familiar with the theories of Gerschler and Dr. Reindell, and he encouraged me to use interval training. I found it to be a worthwhile program that cut more than a minute off my time for 5000 meters and several minutes off my time for 10,000 meters.

In all honesty, a major reason for my improvement was that in the previous year or two, I had doubled the volume of my training to 100 miles a week. All those nighttime runs in the Schwarzwald were having their effect. (That underlines the importance of building a good training base before beginning speedwork.) Nevertheless, interval training definitely was the key to my success. It was my magic workout.

# GAINING AN EDGE
# WITH SLOW QUARTERS

Later, after discharge from the Army, I returned home and began training at Stagg Field, the University of Chicago's track. It is also used by nonstudents, members of coach Ted Haydon's University of Chicago Track Club (U.C.T.C.).

Most runners training at the track—varsity and track club members—were more familiar with fast repeats. Like most American coaches, Haydon trained his runners in this manner. You ran a hard quarter around the track while the coach timed you. You then slowly walked or jogged once more around the track and waited until you caught his eye, so he could time you again for another hard quarter.

Interval training had only begun to penetrate the consciousness of the American distance runner. Other runners who decided to run quarters with me would sometimes become edgy about my seemingly slow pace and sprint ahead. By the end of the workout, they struggled to keep up—*if* they lasted to the end. They had not anticipated the stress imposed by the interval aspect of the workout. Sooner or later, the others became accustomed to this style of training—or found different training partners.

One Chicago runner who shared my enthusiasm for interval training was Gar Williams, who also had recently returned from service in Germany. Haydon used to chuckle at Williams constantly running all those "slow quarters."

Another U.C.T.C. member had placed high in the NCAA championships several years earlier. He trained in the old style, mostly fast repeats. I told Haydon that Williams would probably destroy the other runner later that season when we ran at the National AAU Track-and-Field Championships. Haydon refused to believe me. Sure enough, Williams did what I had predicted. Eventually, Haydon and other American coaches came to appreciate the value of slow quarters. (Williams later won a National AAU marathon title and served a term as president of the Road Runners Club of America.)

The advantage of interval training—and one reason for its appeal to track coaches—is that it allows total control over the workout. It is very systematic, very precise. It is also a good means of charting progress from week to week. If you record workouts in a diary, you can see that this week you ran your quarters in, say, an average of 75.3 seconds, compared to 76.1 last week, or 85.7 two months ago. Don't discount the value of such record-keeping. One reason you succeed with your running is confidence: a belief in yourself and a belief in your training. Interval training on the track can be an important confidence-builder.

Certainly interval training appeals to the computer mind, since by juggling Gerschler's five variables, all sorts of training possibilities present themselves. It is an excellent way of adapting the body to stress, since you push, back off, push some more, back off. It also permits you to train at race pace, and it is an excellent way to learn that pace.

After my introduction to interval training in Germany, I experimented a lot with different patterns. My most frequent workouts were 400s (jogging 400s between) or 200s (jogging 200s between). They could be done very neatly on a 400-meter track outdoors or a 200-meter track indoors. (Of course, back then the tracks, and repetitions, were linear—thus 440 or 220 yards.) Sometimes I used long repetitions and short intervals, such as 1000s with 200s between, or miles with a quarter-mile jog (or 2-minute walk) between. The latter workout I sometimes did with Tom O'Hara, who ran the 1500 for the United States in the 1964 Olympics.

# TOO MUCH OF A GOOD THING

At one point, I experimented with megadoses, where I ran 70 × 300 with a 100 jog, 50 × 400 with 30 seconds between. But I found that sometimes the achievement in the workout outweighed achievements in competition.

Eventually I realized that runners who do too much interval training suffer injuries, possibly from constant stopping and starting and the stress of going around turns on a track. Mental fatigue often was as much a problem as physical fatigue. This was during a period when I, and most other distance runners, did *all* our training on a track. The person who did most to influence us was Mihaly Igloi, the Hungarian coach who defected after the 1956 Olympics and guided the careers of a group of top Americans, including Jim Beatty, Jim Grelle, and Bob Schul. (Beatty and Grelle were among the top milers in the world in the early 1960s; Schul won the 5000 at the 1964 Olympics.)

Igloi was a gifted coach who nevertheless had a reputation (whether deserved or not) for destroying as many runners as he helped with his intensive training methods. Every workout was an interval workout.

Although I had made major improvements by using interval training, I also was prey to overtraining. Today's system of running away from the track—on roads, in the woods—is superior to what I did three decades ago in a frantic effort to succeed.

"The first rule of practice when using genuine interval training," says Brian Mitchell, "is don't use it too often, and don't think it will produce all the goods."

I continue to enjoy occasional interval workouts. My rule now for intervals is *never more than a dozen,* because the purpose for doing such workouts is speed as much as stamina. Now, a typical interval workout for me would be 10 × 400 with 200 jogging between. Finish refreshed.

Save the heroics for race weekends.

# QUESTIONS AND ANSWERS

Here are some commonly asked questions about interval training and their answers.

**Q.** *What distance should you use for your repeats?*

**A.** The longer the interval, the greater the development of your aerobic system, which is important for endurance. (Remember, *interval* refers to the rest or pause in the workout.) The shorter the interval, the greater the development of your anaerobic system, which is important for speed. You need to develop both systems to run fast.

Interval training normally encompasses distances from 200 to 800 meters, although some runners favor longer repetitions. Dr. Jack Daniels described having members of his cross-country team at the State University of New York at Cortland doing what he called "cruise intervals." These were repetitions as long as 2 miles at slightly slower than race pace, with rest intervals of only 30 to 60 seconds. Regardless, the most commonly used distance is 400 meters, because it's a convenient one lap on a track. Start with 400 meters for your repetitions, and vary the distance as you become more comfortable with interval training.

**Q.** *How long should you walk or jog during the rest interval?*

**A.** Gerschler controlled the length of his intervals by measuring pulse rate. A runner whose pulse reached

170 to 180 (90 percent of his MHR) during the repeat
would run again when it dropped to 120 to 130 (70 percent of his MHR).

Very fit runners can turn around and start the next
repeat within 30 seconds of stopping. I watched Sebastian Coe do just that in a workout where he ran 20 ×
200 in 27 to 28 seconds several weeks before winning
the 1500 at the 1984 Olympics. But a more frequent
pattern is to jog the same distance during the interval
as you run during the repeat. For someone running
400-meter reps, this would suggest doing 400-meter jogs
in between. After you become more comfortable with
this form of training, you may want to cut the distance
(thus also the time) of your intervals.

**Q.** *How many repetitions should you run?*
**A.** There are various formulas comparing total volume of
running to race or training distance. Ecker suggested
1½ to 3 times race distance (which probably makes
more sense for middle-distance runners in track than
for distance runners whose race distance is 10-K).
Dr. Daniels suggested a cap of 8 percent of weekly training mileage for cruise interval days: 1½ miles if you run
20 miles a week; 4 miles for those doing 50. Both men
are correct, and both are incorrect. Don't put too much
faith in formulas—including the one I am about to give
you.

A good starting point for runners choosing 400 as the
distance for their repetitions is five intervals. If you
can't do that many, you're probably training too fast. A
good end point is ten intervals. If you can run more than
that, you're probably training too slowly. Runners
choosing 200-meter reps will want to do slightly more;
runners choosing 800-meter reps will want to do less.
But begin cautiously. Dr. Costill warns that too many
runners push hard to make themselves tougher, but instead they push themselves right to the fail point. "The
danger," he says, "is that they begin to develop poor
technique."

**Q.** *How fast should you run your repetitions?*

**A.** Race pace is a convenient (and safe) measuring point for those of us writing books and articles, because that compensates for the fact that those reading our words and following our charts vary greatly, both in ability to race and in ability to endure hard training. The best judge of training pace is a good coach standing beside the track, and even that coach is probably guessing half the time. So begin at a pace comfortably slower than race pace, progressing to that point and somewhat faster.

One frequent recommendation is to choose a pace you would use in a race one-half the distance of the event you're training for. If, for instance, your goal is a fast 10-K, train at a 5-K pace; 5-K runners train at a 3-K pace, and so forth. Scientists claim that training a bit faster than race pace develops the anaerobic system's buffering capacity—that is, its ability to resist stress. Regardless of scientific explanations, slightly faster than race pace is a good end point for interval training. For those using 400s in their interval training, this would mean running up to 5 seconds per quarter faster than you would in a race.

**Q.** *What form of rest should you use during the intervals?*

**A.** There are three types of rest: jogging, walking, or total rest. I would tell one of the freshman members of the track team I helped coach that he had the fastest move of anyone I had seen from the finish line to a seat in the bleachers beside the track: one and a half strides. He was the Michael Jordan of interval resters. Absolute rest doesn't make sense for interval training. You recover too completely, which defeats the purpose of trying to maintain your pulse rate at a continuously high rate (70 to 90 percent of your MHR) during the workout.

Walking is an effective means of rest for those beginning to use this method of training, although some highly trained runners use very short walks between very intense runs. I sometimes walk 100, jog 200, and walk 100 while doing 400-meter repetitions in the early stages of training, but the most popular (and effective) form of interval rest is jogging.

Regardless of which rest you choose, be consistent throughout the workout. Don't begin by jogging at a fast pace between repetitions and finish by having to walk. If that happens, you're jogging too fast or running too many repetitions.

**Q.** *What can you expect from interval training?*

**A.** In an article in *Runner's World,* Ohio State University's David R. Lamb, Ph.D., suggested that the biggest benefit was improved running economy. "If you want to improve your economy at your race pace," Lamb wrote, "you must [train] at or near that pace." Practically every coach would agree with Dr. Lamb.

Interval training also can improve your speed, your endurance, and your pace judgment. But an important, though often overlooked, benefit from interval training is that it improves your ability to concentrate. Because it is very difficult to run consistent times on a track while allowing your mind to drift (as often happens during long runs), you learn to focus your attention on the task at hand. This improved concentration will help with everything you do as a runner.

When I begin doing interval training in the spring, I frequently find my mind drifting on the back stretch during 400s, as though on a long run. And usually I fail to run fast times. As the training period progresses, I discover I can concentrate for longer periods of time, until finally, I run focused the full lap. And my times improve, both on the track and in races. I sometimes wonder how much of that improvement is the result of better conditioning and how much is simply from improved concentration.

**Q.** *How much interval training should you do?*

**A.** Dr. Daniels permits his runners to do no more than one interval session a week. Once a week seems to be a good rule. Those of us from previous generations who did interval training more frequently found it difficult to maintain such an intense level of training without injury. Today, there are too many other interesting and effective training methods available to distance runners, so why train only one way?

**Q.** *Is there a best time of year, time of week, time of day for interval training?*

**A.** Yes. More specific answers depend on your goals and level of ability and conditioning. Interval training works very well when you are getting ready to peak for competition, so if you're seeking fast summer times, early spring is a good time to begin. Weather, of course, may dictate when you can interval train. So will availability of training facilities. If you run long (or race) on weekends, you may want to plan your interval session as far from that effort as possible, thus midweek. Interval training also requires a good warm-up and often more time than a distance run. Most runners probably would fare better doing this workout in late afternoon than in early morning. Do whatever works best for you.

**Q.** *Where should you do interval training?*

**A.** The best venue for interval training is the track. Tracks are convenient because they are marked in 100-, 200-, 300-, and 400-meter segments that make it easier to systemize your training. Tracks certainly are the best choices for those beginning to interval train.

But tracks also offer a form of ambience, since going to the track—driving there, warming up, changing shoes, and so on—signals to the body: "Okay, today's the day we run fast!" Also, training partners often are more easily available at the track. But once you learn the basics of interval training and discover you can measure your level of effort by time, by pulse, or even by perceived exertion, you can move your interval training anywhere: roads, woods, wherever. At some point, such training blends into fartlek (which I'll cover in chapter 10), but don't worry about that yet.

**Q.** *How can you guard against overtraining and injuries?*

**A.** Coach Dellinger states that you should be able to run the last repetition at the same pace as the first—or faster. "If it's a real struggle," he warns, "you should start your next workout at a slower pace, or increase the recovery." Dellinger also suggests that runners use training flats, not track spikes, even for running on a track. (The one exception to this would be on a rainy day, when a wet track might be slippery.) There is no foolproof way of avoiding overtraining or injury, but if you approach your interval work with the idea that it should be an intense workout—not a *punishing* one— you will find this form of training both more enjoyable and successful.

Finally, although interval training is a very precise and scientific means of improving your running ability, don't become bogged down with numbers. "Vary the program," advises Dellinger. "Do different sets of intervals, different distances, and experiment with recovery times." Good advice from a good coach. Although all the experts agree that interval training may be the most effective type of training devised, it is not the only type, or even the best. Use it judiciously if you want to become a fast runner.

# Chapter 9

# SPRINTS, SURGES, STRIDES

## RACING TACTICS THAT WORK

**D**oes a competitor in 5-K and 10-K events need to worry about pure speed, flat speed, absolute speed—or whatever you want to call sprinting as hard as you can? And where do these decisive bursts come from?

After all, in races of those lengths, victory often goes to the athlete capable of controlling and *maintaining* his or her speed over the full distance. Milers may rely on their kick to win, but 10-K runners more often achieve victory by pushing hard in the fourth and fifth miles, working at top speed and sustaining that pace to the end. And most 10-K runners back in the pack compete against only their own previous personal achievements as they reach the kicking field, the last 100 meters.

# TAMING TIME
# WITH A FINAL KICK

Regardless of position in the field, almost any runner who has entered the last stretch and glanced above the finish line to see the digital clock relentlessly ticking away—55 . . . 56 . . . 57 . . . 58 . . . 59—certainly hopes at that moment to have a kick.

At the 1990 Berlin Marathon, I saw exactly that sort of countdown as I neared the line. A quick spurt brought me across in a precise 3:09:59. That's far below my PR. I finished 3,711th overall, 49th in my age group. Big deal, you say. Okay, but when the results booklet eventually arrived by mail, I took pride in the fact that I was the last runner listed among the block of runners finishing between 3:00:00 and 3:10:00. I'll take my victories where I can get them.

Sure, we'd all like a better kick. Regardless of race position, we'd like the ability to take it out of cruise control over the last 100, put the pedal to the metal, and raise a cheer from the crowd as we steam past some guy we've been trailing for the last 3 miles.

Of course, grumblers will say that if you had properly paced yourself during the full length of the race, you would have fully utilized your energy and not have had anything left for a kick. The goal, it seems, is to finish each race totally spent, knowing that you could not possibly have obtained one more stride from your depleted muscles.

That may be a noteworthy goal for those seeking Olympic medals, but most of us finish races having not quite squeezed the last drop from the lemon. Even the best of us operate somewhere around the 98th or 99th percentile when it comes to extracting energy. Usually, we can reach down and find an untapped reserve. By driving our arms, by lifting our knees, we can move fast at the finish. In doing so, we are not necessarily utilizing energy or activating muscles that might have better been used earlier. We are actually tapping different energy systems and utilizing different muscles—sprinter's muscles—that otherwise go unused.

# THE 3 S's OF SUCCESS

But apart from any advantage in having pure speed to utilize in the kicking field, such speed is important to use throughout the length of your race. If you can teach yourself to be a better sprinter and to be a more efficient and economical runner, you will develop a capability to run fast.

One way to improve pure speed is with the three S's: sprints, strides, and surges.

Sprints and strides, at least, are variations on the same theme. Different coaches might define them differently. Both are runs of short distances, a straightaway on a track or a short fairway on a golf course (about 100 meters). A *sprint* usually means just that: an all-out sprint for the distance. A *stride* is somewhat slower, usually faster than race pace but not all-out (although you might reach full speed during at least a brief portion of the distance). A *surge* is a fast burst: a sprint or stride thrown into the middle of a distance workout.

Confused? That's understandable, because the difference between the three S's is not great. Let's discuss sprints, strides, and surges at somewhat greater length.

# STRAIGHTAWAYS TO FASTER TIMES

A subtle difference exists between sprints and the two forms of speedwork covered in previous chapters: repeats and interval training. When I run repeats, I run nearly flat out, fully anaerobic, but with maximum rest. In doing interval training, I usually run under control but with less rest, a mixture of anaerobic and aerobic work.

A sprint is running flat out, but over a shorter distance, so as to stress (and train) the muscles more than the cardiovascular system. Sprints, like repeats, are totally anaerobic, although if enough of them are run with jogging in between, the effect may be similar to that of interval training. But that defeats the purpose of sprints, which, at least the way I do them, occupy a middle ground between repeats and intervals.

What's the scientific rationale for going faster in practice than you would in a race? I asked that question of Ball State's Dr. David Costill.

Dr. Costill mentioned technique—the ability to run efficiently at a very fast pace—then added: "I've never been convinced that you develop greater energy production for the anaerobic system by doing anaerobic training. That system can be taught to work quite well when only moderately trained, such as through interval training. The real advantage of running faster is that you get stronger."

Most track athletes run sprints on the track. They sometimes call them "straightaways," because a convenient way to do them is to sprint one straightaway, jog around the turn, and sprint the next straightaway. Other runners prefer to walk between sprints. They will walk, stop, turn around, walk, jog, and sprint back in the other direction. Or they walk back to where they started and sprint back in the same direction. When I include sprints in my warm-up before a track race or even a road race, I usually stop and walk back halfway, then jog to where I start my next sprint. It's a matter of personal preference and convenience as to how and where you run your sprints.

Usually I prefer running sprints on soft surfaces. If the track is hard asphalt, similar to that at most high schools, you may be better off running your sprints on the grass inside the track. But test the softness and smoothness of any surface before you run hard on it. Uneven surfaces are death to sprinters.

More often, I use the fairway of a golf course. I live a half-mile from Long Beach Country Club, a private club that, fortunately, does not have a fence around it. During summer months, I arrive early in the morning before the golfers, sometimes even before sunrise. It's a cool, pleasant part of the day. There are several fairways that I favor for sprints, depending on where the greenkeepers are mowing that day.

I run from tree to tree rather than any specific distance.

Distance is irrelevant. Time doesn't matter. Regardless of where you run your sprints, on a golf course or at the track, I consider it useless to time yourself for any distance shorter than 200 meters. Time differences in tenths of a second from one sprint to another mean little. If you're timing yourself, you're diverting your concentration by clicking your watch on and off. Focus your attention on running as swiftly and smoothly as you can for as far as you can, and worry about times at some other point in your training.

## *PICK YOUR DISTANCE CAREFULLY*

How far should you run your sprints? I recommend confining yourself to a distance between 60 and 100 meters—about the length of a track straightaway, a fraction of a golf fairway. In a 100-meter dash, most sprinters reach peak speed about 60 meters into the race and actually decelerate somewhat before crossing the line. In a 200-meter dash, victory often goes not to the fastest sprinter but to the one who shows the least deceleration. When Olympic great Carl Lewis ran his fastest 200-meter races, he seemed to cruise around the turn and ignite the afterburners once he hit the straightaway. Actually, Lewis simply maintained his form and speed better than the other 200-meter sprinters. Said another way, they slowed down faster. Pure speed—to use coach Robert Vaughan's term—occurs in the first 60 to 100 meters of any sprint, whether race or workout.

As an example, at the 1987 World Track & Field Championships in Rome, Canada's Ben Johnson defeated Lewis in the 100 meters, running what was then considered a world record: 9.83 to Lewis's 9.93. An analysis of their times at each 10-meter point during the race shows that both Johnson and Lewis attained peak speed between 50 and 70 meters (each running 0.83 for two consecutive 10-meter segments). Then they faded ever so slightly over the remaining 30 meters, during which Lewis ran 0.02 faster than his rival. (See the table on page 122.) But this was not enough for him to compensate for the 0.08 he lost in the first 10 meters to Johnson's explosive start. Unfortunately, when Johnson tested positive for steroids after win-

## Johnson and Lewis Splits

| Distance (in meters) | Ben Johnson Time (in seconds) | Split | Carl Lewis Time (in seconds) | Split |
|---|---|---|---|---|
| 10 | 1.86 | 1.86 | 1.96 | 1.96 |
| 20 | 2.87 | 1.01 | 2.97 | 1.03 |
| 30 | 3.80 | 0.93 | 3.92 | 0.95 |
| 40 | 4.66 | 0.86 | 4.77 | 0.85 |
| 50 | 5.55 | 0.89 | 5.67 | 0.90 |
| 60 | 6.38 | 0.83 | 6.50 | 0.83 |
| 70 | 7.21 | 0.90 | 7.33 | 0.83 |
| 80 | 8.11 | 0.89 | 8.23 | 0.90 |
| 90 | 8.98 | 0.87 | 9.09 | 0.86 |
| 100 | 9.83 | 0.85 | 9.93 | 0.84 |

ning the 100 meters at the 1988 Olympic Games in South Korea, he lost credit for the 9.83 record set at Rome as well as the 9.79 run in Seoul. He was stripped of his victories.

Assuming the 10-meter splits taken in Rome to be accurate, and assuming further that this reflects the relative ability of *all* sprinters (or distance runners trying to be sprinters), you will achieve peak velocity between 50 and 100 meters. If you run much farther, you're training for something other than pure speed. You begin to train for speed endurance, the ability to maintain speed rather than to increase it. Regardless of what the above data tells us, 100 meters is a good distance for doing sprints—or strides.

Ron Gunn, Southwestern Michigan College's track coach, uses an even shorter distance for what he calls "NFL speed drags." Gunn has his team run 40-meter sprints, the same distance pro football teams use when they test promising rookies. They test at that distance because anything longer measures something beyond pure speed.

Gunn stands two of his runners on the line in a power start position: left foot forward, right foot back, right arm high, left arm cocked behind. He shouts "Go!" and they drag-race each other, just like two hot rods on a drag strip at maximum speed. It's a good speed exercise for college kids to do, although I'm not sure I would recommend it for older runners because of the high potential for injury from using a dynamic start.

## MORE ISN'T ALWAYS BETTER

Indeed, you need to use speedwork cautiously and judiciously. It helps if you have a good coach looking over your shoulder when you train. Many years ago, when I was experimenting with my training, when *more* seemed to equate with *best,* I used to go to the cinder track and do massive quantities of flat-out sprints. I would do 10 × 100, jogging the same distance between, then walk 100 before another set of 10. Following another brief rest, I would run 5 × 200, trying for under 30 seconds each, jogging 200 between. Then another 10 × 100. By now I was wobbly-legged. Finally, I'd do one last set of 10—fast again, because I was starting to recover after the killer 200s.

It is the sort of workout that looks good in your diary. But I was dropping out of marathon races about the same time, probably because I was overtrained and had failed to develop my ability to run at race pace.

I no longer run sprints for either punishment or endurance. I run them for speed and to stretch my muscles. Fred Wilt, now the cooordinator of coaches' education for TAC, trained me in the mid-1960s, a period when I recorded my fastest times. He felt that distance runners should run sprints at least once a week for three reasons: (1) to develop muscular strength, (2) to accustom the cardiovascular system to tolerating a much higher level of effort than normally encountered at race pace, and (3) to develop anaerobic endurance. I still consider his reasoning to be sound. Of the three reasons he suggested, I consider developing strength to be the most important.

## SPEED THERAPY FOR YOUR MUSCLES

What is the difference between sprints and strides? That's easy. Strides are simply slow sprints. How much slower? That's as much in the mind as in the muscle. At the top end, a stride could be almost full speed, but a notch below. One variation Wilt suggested is to gradually accelerate to top speed at around 50 or 60 meters, then to gradually decelerate. Gunn uses a similar acceleration but has his runners hit 100 percent at 100 meters. These are effective methods of combining sprints and strides. Try them and see how they feel.

I most often run this mutant form of speedwork as therapeutic repair work, sometimes after a long workout or on what I would classify as an "easy" day. To me, strides are another form of stretching. I also use strides as part of my warm-up before racing, or before training involving more serious speedwork. Before running repeats or interval training, I do sprints or strides, more often the latter. Actually, if I'm doing eight straightaways as part of a warm-up, the first three or four will be strides (gradually increasing in tempo), with one or two sprints before closing with one or two strides.

## A DRILL FOR RECOVERY

Many distance runners include long runs—those Sunday morning 20-milers—as part of their regular training. Often, running a long, slow distance leaves your legs stiff and tight. That's one reason why distance runners lose flexibility, an essential component for running fast. As part of my recovery from long distance, I often would take a short, second workout later in the day that consisted mainly of strides. Now that I'm older (and perhaps wiser), I'll do a workout of strides later in the week.

One of the main reasons I do strides is to undo some of the damage, such as stiffness, that results from my long or hard workouts and to prepare myself for further fast training.

Remember that. While sprints build strength and speed, strides function best for recovery, so that you can use other workouts to build strength and speed.

For me, a typical recovery workout featuring strides would be to jog from my home to the golf course, taking a slightly extended route so that I arrive there after covering about 1 mile. I stretch under an evergreen tree beside the first fairway, dangling from a low branch as one of my stretches. Then I jog over to the 18th fairway, where I stride through eight or more 130-yarders (tree to tree). Following that, I jog home by a slightly longer route. This gives me a workout of maybe 3 miles. Poor for the diary, but good for the body.

Generally, the first stride is little more than a bowlegged shuffle as I work out the kinks from my previous hard workouts. More often, I walk rather than jog between. By the time I have completed eight strides, I usually am able to run a respectably fast pace, though still not a sprint. I avoid punishing myself and quit early. Usually as I jog back home, I run much more relaxed than I did on the way out. I finish refreshed. There's nothing scientific about the workout, but it feels good.

## A GREAT WARM-UP

Strides also form part of my prerace warm-up (as I covered in chapter 4), which usually begins with a mile or two of jogging. After some relaxed stretching, I do two to four strides of 75 meters or so at a pace that seems to feel comfortable. After more jogging, I am ready to race. This warm-up is a holdover from my track days, and it works for me.

Dr. Jack Daniels is among the respected coaches and physiologists who recommend strides as an important regimen on so-called light training days. Dr. Owen Anderson, discussing Dr. Daniels's training in his publication *Running Research News,* described a method of doing strides:

Midway through or at the end of your easy run, run for about 100 meters at close to your mile pace. (Don't sprint; try to run comfortably.) Following each stride, jog lightly for 15 to 20 seconds before commencing the next stride. After five strides have been completed, walk around for a couple of minutes until you feel completely rested and recovered, and then do a second set of five strides to finish your striding for the day. The purpose for strides is to reinforce the mechanics of race pace (you get ten chances to run at race speed) and perk up what might be a boring training day. At first, try doing strides on one or two of your easy training days each week; if all goes well, you can increase the number of days you do strides.

Learning to run strides is simple. It takes about 15 seconds of instruction for me to teach a new member of my cross-country team how to do strides. Experiment with this form of speed training and see how easy it is.

# BREAKAWAYS FOR THE MIDDLE OF THE RACE

"Surge" is the third S, but surges fit uncomfortably beside sprints and strides. Some runners might argue that surges do not qualify as pure speed, and they probably are right— except that while you are surging, you usually are moving at a very fast pace.

What are surges? They are fast sprints thrown into the middle of a long run. Coach Gunn refers to surges as "break 'em drills," since by surging in the middle of a race, you often can break your opponent. He has his runners wait until the final third of a workout before doing surges. "If they do them too early, you'll lose them for the rest of the run," says Gunn.

I often include surges in the middle of a hard, fast run. For example, while doing a fast 10-miler, I might begin at an 8-minute-mile pace. But after a few miles of gradual acceleration, I'll reach a steady pace near 6 minutes, holding it for several miles. During the middle of this workout, if I'm feeling strong, I might attempt several surges—I pick up the pace to faster than 6 minutes, hold it for several hundred yards, then ease slightly, only to surge again. Usually by the tenth and final mile in such a workout, I have slowed to 8 minutes, although not necessarily by choice. Obviously, the pace increment for different runners would vary according to ability. A world-class runner might surge to near 4-minute pace; a runner of lesser ability might run surges near 8 minutes.

On other occasions, I will run long surges, changing pace

several times during a run of 1 hour's duration. One example is when I run with the cross-country team in the Indiana Dunes State Park over a figure-eight course that includes what we call the ridge trail, a wooded bluff high over the beach. We begin by running 10 minutes to a point in the woods where we stop and stretch, then head up onto the ridge. The trail winds back and forth, dipping and diving, forcing the runner to make constant surges, a series of sprints or strides thrown into the middle of what is essentially a long run. At the end of the ridge, we relax, coast, gather forces, and let gravity carry us down a sand dune. We back off the pace for a mile or two before turning onto a trail and boardwalk crossing a swamp, which coaxes us into a long surge before returning to our starting point.

Wait a minute, you say: Aren't you training speed endurance rather than pure speed? Many forms of speed training overlap. They lead into each other. They complement each other. In actuality, we train using a blend of repeats and interval training. The easy run between ridge and swamp serves as our interval. It's also a form of fartlek, which leads us to the next chapter and what many might call the most delightful, and most demanding, type of speedwork.

# Chapter 10

# *FARTLEK*

## *A TIME-TESTED TREASURE*

**T**he late Swedish coach Gosta Holmer once said: "It is not the fixed courses that make a professor out of a student, but the student's spirit of exploration. It is the same thing with an athlete."

Holmer, who coached his country's Olympic team, was the inventor of *fartlek,* a Swedish term that roughly translates to "speed play." If you took repeats, repetitions, intervals, strides, and sprints and dumped them in a bowl and mixed them all together, you would have fartlek. It is a very effective, and satisfying, form of training when done properly.

In an article in *Athletics Journal,* Paul A. Smith described fartlek as "a continuous overdistance run with numerous faster-paced interval runs interspersed, until the runner feels tired, but not exhausted." Smith claimed that because fartlek existed in the mind of the runner as a form of play, it deemphasized the feeling or perception of fatigue.

Fartlek was first used successfully by the two great Swedish milers of the 1940s, Gunnar Haag and Arne Anderson. It consists of fast, medium, and slow running over a variety of distances, depending on the terrain.

In a typical fartlek workout, you pick some landmark such as a tree or a bush and sprint to it, then jog until you've recovered. Select another landmark a shorter—or longer—distance away, and run to it at a faster—or slower—pace. The distance and pace are up to you. The *most* important skill for this drill is listening to your body. Sometimes you may want to jog more. Add some sprints or strides, and maybe even walk, as the mood develops. "An athlete runs as he feels," says the University of Oregon's Bill Dellinger. "A fartlek training session can be the hardest workout a runner does all week, or it can be the easiest." It depends on how you structure the workout and how long you stay out. Coach Dellinger calls fartlek "instinctive."

"In order to be a good distance runner," he adds, "you have to build strength and endurance, learn race pace, and practice race tactics. Fartlek training can incorporate all of these essential elements into a single workout."

# FAST RESULTS, FEW INJURIES

In a *Runner's World* article, Dellinger described a study on the benefits of fartlek vs. the benefits of interval training. It included 30 distance runners and was conducted by a graduate student at the University of Oregon. One group ran fartlek, a second group did interval training, and a third group did a combination of both workouts. After a year's training, during which time the runners were tested every two weeks, the fartlek group got into shape the slowest and had the poorest early results. But the runners benefited from fewer injuries. The interval group, on the other hand, had the best early marks but also suffered the most injuries. Perhaps because they suffered fewer injuries—and therefore trained more consistently—the fartlek runners began to outperform the interval group toward the end of the study.

But the lesson to be learned came from the third group. This group's performance shone because the runners *combined* interval training with fartlek. They had better results and fewer injuries.

Clearly, fartlek can play an effective role in almost any runner's training, particularly in the area of speedwork, if it's combined with other methods.

# FARTLEK FOR EVERYONE

Holmer felt that fartlek, done correctly, could be practiced three to five times a week. He recommended running uphill no more than twice a week, preferably on Mondays and Thursdays. "Fartlek brings us back to the games of our childhood," said Holmer. "The runner is forced to explore."

The Swedish coach operated in an era when competitive runners were only young and highly skilled athletes. (The 10-K hadn't even been invented yet.) Times have changed.

## FOR BEGINNERS

So the question is: Can today's runners of more average ability benefit from Holmer's fartlek training?

Yes. The Atlanta Track Club, with 60 volunteer coaches, offers a special program for its members—any member of the club can obtain qualified coaching by simply requesting it. Among the volunteers is Mary Reed, who prefers to work with beginning runners, usually women, on a one-to-one basis.

Once her students have reached the point in their training where they can benefit from speedwork, Reed, instead of taking them to the track, teaches them how to do fartlek. Utilizing a ¾-mile loop around a reservoir, she has them alternate between running slow and running easy for non-specific distances and times.

"I find that many beginners, who didn't participate in sports in high school, are intimidated by the track," says Reed. "The track, they think, is where only fast runners go. They're afraid that they'll be the slowest runner and intimidated by being left in a cloud of dust. Instead of going to the track at 4:30 in the morning, when nobody else is there, we simply do fartlek."

Reed uses fartlek to convince the beginners that speedwork can benefit their running. First she has them run a 5-K race. Then they use fartlek in their training regimen for three or four weeks before they measure themselves with another 5-K race.

"With beginning runners," says Reed, "they'll often improve from race to race just because they've had another month of training. But when you mix in fartlek, the improvement often is dramatic."

## FOR TEAM MEMBERS

Different coaches, of course, interpret fartlek in different ways. At the College of the Holy Cross in Massachusetts, W. H. (Skip) O'Connor designed a program based on time rather than miles that included what he described as bursts, lifts, steady strides, specific hill attacks, fast openers, fast closers, passing pickups, and bolts. Bursts were 50-yard sprints on a flat area, a half dozen or so within a 5-minute time span. These were prearranged sprints performed by his entire team at a signal from the leader. Bolts, however, were sudden and unexpected sprints by various individuals, who had been instructed by O'Connor to uncork them several times during the workout.

## FOR THE SELF-COACHED

The Soviet Union's A. Yakimov, as he wrote in *Track Technique,* felt that the length of the fast runs, along with the length and form of rest, should be determined by the athlete according to how he feels physically. The important ingredient is constant change of pace. Yakimov's formula was as follows:

**1.** Light running for 5 to 10 minutes as a warm-up. A fast, even run for 1 to 2 kilometers.

**2.** A brisk walk for 5 minutes.

**3.** Light, even running with short accelerations (50 to 60 meters) until you sense some fatigue.

**4.** Light running with the occasional inclusion of four to five fast strides. (These are like sudden surges in a race.)

**5.** Fast uphill running for 1 minute.

Yakimov stressed that at the end of the workout, you should feel not fatigue, but rather enthusiasm. "Fartlek is not a 'carefree' system as is sometimes thought. It is not to be used only as a rest from hard workouts. It demands no less of physical and psychological strength than any other method."

# RUNNING FREE

To simply copy the formulas of Holmer, O'Connor, or Yakimov (or any other coach) would rob fartlek of its greatest advantage—its spirit of free play. Coach Dellinger believes that it is the intentional "vagueness" of fartlek that makes it less stressful than other forms of hard running.

Merrill Noden described fartlek in an article titled "Playing on the Run" in *The Runner.* "In any interval session—on or off the track—you are measuring two variables: the distance you run and the time it takes," he wrote. "Real fartlek always leaves one or both of these variables unmeasured." As a result, said Noden, you make it impossible to pass judgment on your effort.

As such, fartlek lends itself to the cross-country setting, because training venues away from the track are almost always unmarked and undefined. Yes, courses on which runners race frequently come accompanied by mileposts that cannot be totally ignored; but typically, when runners run off-road, whether woods or golf course, they run free. It becomes easier, then, for terrain to dictate training. A hill encountered becomes an excuse for a short sprint. A smooth straightaway offers an opportunity for a controlled fast run. Soft footing makes it necessary to slow down.

The principles of fartlek do not need to be reserved for special days. You can work it into most any workout. On your distance days, you can throw in surges or sprints when the spirit moves you.

One winter's day, for example, I was running with Liz Galaviz, the top runner on my cross-country team. Snow was on the ground, so we ran a 5-mile course through city streets at an undefined pace.

Liz was feeling strong, so midway through the run, I found myself hanging on to her fast pace. At an intersection where we normally would have turned right, I pointed her straight up a hill about 100 to 150 meters in length. We ran the hill side-by-side, and I could hear her breathing become labored. When the hill leveled off and started down, we eased the pace to recover.

"I just did that to be mean," I said.

Liz smiled, "I know."

But I did that, as she realized, to toughen her for running short track races later that spring. It was a classic fartlek move, but one that had been inserted within the framework of what had started out as a relatively easy distance run. It was the perfect "speed play."

# Chapter 11

# UP-TEMPO RUNNING

## A PROGRAM FOR ULTIMATE AEROBIC POWER

**O**n a clear Saturday afternoon during the Thanksgiving weekend, I set out from my house and ran westward along Lake Shore Drive, toward Michigan City. It was 48°F, perfect weather for running. After covering several blocks, I jogged down a set of wooden stairs and clambered across a breakwater to reach the beach.

Storms from the Northwest over a period of several days had sent waves pounding against the beach. On such days, I run elsewhere. But when the winds die and the waves recede, it leaves a perfect surface for running, similar to Daytona Beach in Florida, where they once raced cars on the hard sand.

Hard, but yielding. Better than even a rubberized track

for speedy workouts. Perfect for what on that day in late November became an anaerobic threshold run, what I prefer to call "wind running."

I had not planned to run hard, because my legs still were somewhat sore from a 10-K race on a hilly course two days before (the Turkey Trot in Niles, Michigan). But the perfect conditions forced me into a gradual acceleration almost against my will. My body told me to go, so I went.

Within 32 minutes, I reached the breakwater outside the harbor in Michigan City, not fast when you consider the distance is nearly 4 miles. That's barely an 8-minute-mile pace, several minutes per mile slower than I had raced two days earlier. But toward the middle of that workout, I had begun to run very fast indeed.

I pushed hard. My knees rose. My stride grew long. My arms swung perceptibly faster. My rate of breathing increased, although it was not yet labored. My eyes focused straight ahead on the carpet of wet sand that stretched in front of me. I became oblivious to the scenery left and right: the blue of the lake, the faded green of the dune grass with its row of cottages beyond. I could feel the wind in my hair.

## SWIFT MOVEMENTS

The wind would not register on any meteorological charts that afternoon; it was generated only by my swift movements along the sand. This is why I run. Not for victories. Not for trophies. Not for prize money, precious little of which is available for a man in my age group anyway. Certainly not for glory. I run because I love the sensation of running fast. The wind in my hair.

I can also tell you that my workout—not entirely by design—was guaranteed to improve my level of conditioning, so that the next time I went to a starting line, it would allow me to run faster. I had been beaten by 30 seconds at Niles by another runner in my age group, Harry Tellman of Holland, Michigan. That particular workout was not designed to defeat Tellman the next time we stepped to a line together, but it could have that effect.

In point of fact, I was engaging in a workout that different coaches and exercise physiologists describe with different terms. It's perhaps best known among readers of training articles in running magazines as *anaerobic threshold training,* or *A.T. running.* Peter Snell, the Olympic champion turned scientist, told me he prefers "lactate threshold training." John Babington, Lynn Jennings's coach, refers to it as "up-tempo aerobic running." Ron Gunn, coach at Southwestern Michigan College, describes such workouts as "F.C.R.'s," for fast continuous runs. That's a term I've often favored, but I've also heard such runs described as "Conconis," after Francesco Conconi, Ph.D., the exercise physiologist from Ferrara and adviser for many of Italy's top distance runners who helped popularize this form of training.

Coach Robert Vaughan talks about the "deflection point"—the mythical dotted line around 90 percent of maximum heart rate (MHR). If you run above that, say at 91 percent, lactic acid begins to accumulate in your muscles and inevitably causes you to crash. But run just below that dotted line, say at 89 percent, and all sorts of marvelous things happen to your level of conditioning.

Dr. Jack Daniels wrote about this effect in *Runner's World* in an article called "Cruise Control," billed on the cover of that magazine as "The Biggest Training Discovery in 50 Years." On reflection, this was only a slight exaggeration. Dr. Daniels called the workout "tempo running." His term for interval running at that same pace, "cruise intervals," immediately found a place in the runner's lexicon. For the next several months, I encountered the term frequently during discussions with other runners, all of whom seemed to have embraced cruise control.

# THE SECRETS OF THE ANAEROBIC THRESHOLD

Let's talk about anaerobic threshold (which I mentioned in chapter 2), what it means, and where it exists as a function of human performance. Ball State's Dr. David Costill has described anaerobic threshold as the point during exercise when the metabolism supposedly switches from an aerobic to an anaerobic state, when the body's demand for oxygen exceeds its ability to produce it. Dr. Costill says: "Since lactic acid tends to be produced by the muscles when they are unable to acquire sufficient oxygen to produce energy aerobically, its accumulation in the blood is considered to be a good indicator of the pace that the runner can tolerate during long runs."

The term *anaerobic threshold* was coined in 1972 by California physiologist Karl Wasserman. He measured the blood acidity of individuals undergoing progressively intense exercise and noted that at a certain point, the blood acidity increased suddenly. Wasserman suggested that this was the anaerobic threshold, the point at which anaerobic metabolism was initiated. Not all scientists would agree with this assessment today, although in drafting training plans, it becomes convenient to assume that there exists a "red line" above which you do not stray long if you plan to continue running.

The biochemical mechanisms that produce glycogen, which fuels the muscles, are complex and require various fuel sources. When exercise is moderate, aerobic metabolism predominates. Glycogen is broken down completely. Oxygen combines with freed hydrogen ions to produce water and carbon dioxide, which are easily carried off.

*Aerobic* is defined as "in the presence of oxygen," meaning that sufficient oxygen is delivered by the cardiovascular system to maintain a steady state of energy production through the breakdown of glycogen. Aerobic activity generally is associated with slow speeds, jogging, or running long distance.

But a new system kicks in after exercise increases in intensity, so the demands for energy exceed the rate at which oxygen can be delivered. Glycogen is broken down *an*aerobically, but the process is not complete. Lactic acid, as well as free hydrogen ions, accumulate.

*Anaerobic* is defined as "without oxygen," meaning that exercise is so intense that the cardiovascular system cannot provide sufficient oxygen for efficient energy production. The waste products cannot be carried away rapidly enough. Consequently, lactic acid accumulates in the muscles and bloodstream and eventually makes it impossible to run farther. Anaerobic activity generally is associated with sprinting, running distances shorter than 1500 meters.

But the questions are: When does aerobic activity become anaerobic activity? When does a jog become a sprint, at least in perceived effort? Where is the red line in running? How can we identify and use this red line—or anaerobic threshold—to plan our training runs?

# RUNNING CLOSE TO THE RED LINE

Presumably an athlete capable of determining his or her anaerobic threshold would have an advantage both in training and in competition. That runner, perhaps you, could train at a pace just below that threshold, permitting him to maximize his effort and energy without suffering from the accumulation of lactic acid. Could that knowledge also be applied in a race? I'm less convinced of that, since in races between 5-K and 10-K, well-trained runners eventually must enter the twilight zone above the red line. But certainly anything that increases body awareness makes you a better runner.

Unfortunately, theory (and what scientists perceive in the laboratory) does not always match reality. In talking about an anaerobic threshold, many runners probably think there is a certain speed (or pace) below which all activity is aerobic and above which all activity is anaerobic. They might visualize 400 meters run in 90 seconds (6-minute pace) as aerobic and in 45 seconds as anaerobic, with the threshold somewhere in between.

This is not true, as Dr. Costill quickly points out: "In reality, there exists a continuum between aerobic and anaerobic activity. Pure aerobic activity probably does not exist in athletics. It is achieved only at rest or during mild walking. Even in golf, the explosive golf swing is anaerobic."

And even while functioning at a very, very low energy level—say 50 percent of your MHR—you are exercising both aerobically *and* anaerobically. You provide oxygen, but not as much as the system demands. As you increase your exercise intensity—go from 60 to 70 to 80 percent of your MHR, as I did during my run on the beach—more of your energy conversion becomes anaerobic. Eventually, you reach that point of muscular breakdown where you can run no longer. Scientists induce this in the laboratory by running a subject on a treadmill, gradually tilting the angle until he no longer can keep pace. For a sprinter struggling down the straightaway in the 400 meters, it certainly does seem as though the track is being tilted just before the finish line.

Scientists have studied aerobic energy production since the early nineteenth century. Since then, aerobic capacity is relatively easier to measure by standard laboratory techniques, including analysis of blood and gas exchanges. Although scientists recently have begun to give more attention to anaerobic energy, it is less readily measurable.

One problem with drawing conclusions about the so-called anaerobic threshold from blood and gas measurements is that not all of the action takes place in the blood or immediately affects the oxygen transport systems. The real action occurs in the muscle, and the increase in blood acidity occurs after the fact—how long after we do not know. It is the acid level in the muscle that affects the muscle's capability to contract—and your ability to run.

The point of this is that the term *anaerobic threshold,* as it is currently being used by many exercise physiologists and interpreted to the public, is probably a misnomer. To obtain precise measurement, we would need to monitor the acidity within the muscle, no easy task even with the new noninvasive measuring devices available to exercise scientists today. Even the pulse watch I frequently wear in training allows me to make only an educated guess as to when I am approaching my anaerobic threshold. I assume that red line to be at 90 percent of my MHR, 133 out of a max of 150. But my A.T. point could be somewhat higher or somewhat lower. One factor is my relative fitness level. The A.T. for an untrained person might be below 50 percent; someone highly trained could red-line above 90 percent, although probably not too much beyond.

After a race in Minnesota, I spoke with a runner of average ability from Minneapolis who had visited a fitness center to have his anaerobic threshold tested. Preparing for an important ultramarathon race, he was sparing no expense. The test involved having him pedal on an exercise bicycle while having his air volume and blood lactate monitored. The tester eventually informed the runner that his anaerobic threshold was 130 beats per minute.

That value (72 percent) seemed rather low for a well-conditioned runner, since he reported his MHR at 180. But the center testers had failed to measure that value; they had merely estimated by using a standard formula. There are two formulas used to estimate MHR. One is to take the number 220 and subtract your age. In my case, this predicts a max of 160. Another popular method is to take the number 200 and subtract half your age. This predicts a max for me of 170. In actuality, my max is 153, and it has been within a few beats of that level for the last 20 years, even when the so-called formulas were predicting much higher values.

Formulas are fine for predicting average values, but not everybody is average. I told the runner that this was a classic case of "garbage in, garbage out." Although the fitness center seemed to be utilizing the latest space-age measuring devices, they lost any chance of a careful measurement of his anaerobic threshold by utilizing a probably flawed estimate of his MHR.

I quizzed the runner further about his training, which he monitored with a pulse watch. He and his regular training partner frequently go for 2-hour runs, maintaining a steady pulse rate between 140 and 145, which would mean around 80 percent of maximum. "Then your threshold is probably somewhere around 150," I suggested. I ended by telling the runner he should quit trying to be too scientific and simply train the way he feels.

# PULSE TRAINING AND
# THE A.T. WORKOUT

Nevertheless, I must confess that it's often fun to imbue your training with at least a certain level of pseudoscience. And measuring your training can provide motivation. During the workout on the beach I described earlier, I was able to measure my cardiovascular response with precise accuracy because I wore a pulse watch. A strap around my chest contained a radio transmitter that beamed signals from my beating heart to the watch. I could glance down at my wrist and obtain an instant pulse reading, or after returning home, I could review the pulse record of that workout—sort of an instant replay of how my heart performed.

The record of that workout follows. My watch recorded my pulse every 60 seconds. Keep in mind that I have a low pulse, my maximum being near 150.

## WARM-UP

*Time:* 13:00
*Percentage of total run:* 20
*Action:* Easy beginning
*Percentage of MHR:* 65 to 75
*Perceived exertion:* Fairly light to somewhat hard
*Pulse readings:*

| | |
|---|---|
| 1. — | 8. 108 |
| 2. — | 9. 105 |
| 3. — | 10. 109 |
| 4. 95 | 11. 115 |
| 5. 98 | 12. 111 |
| 6. 99 | 13. 112 |
| 7. 107 | |

*Comments:* Missing numbers reflect inaccurate early readings. Stiff after race two days before. Not yet certain how hard I want to run.

## BUILDUP

*Time:* 13:00
*Percentage of total run:* 20
*Action:* Gentle acceleration
*Percentage of MHR:* 75 to 80
*Perceived exertion:* Hard
*Pulse readings:*

| | |
|---|---|
| 1. 116 | 8. 118 |
| 2. 118 | 9. 118 |
| 3. 113 | 10. 117 |
| 4. 115 | 11. 117 |
| 5. 119 | 12. 118 |
| 6. 118 | 13. 118 |
| 7. 119 | |

*Comments:* Began to loosen up. Good running conditions—both weather and surface—prompted me to speed up.

## A.T. SEGMENT

*Time:* 24:00
*Percentage of total run:* 40
*Action:* Controlled speed run
*Percentage of MHR:* 80 to 90
*Perceived exertion:* Very hard
*Pulse readings:*

| | | |
|---|---|---|
| 1. 122 | 9. 125 | 17. 129 |
| 2. 122 | 10. 128 | 18. 132 |
| 3. 122 | 11. 127 | 19. 133 |
| 4. 120 | 12. 127 | 20. 133 |
| 5. 123 | 13. 130 | 21. 130 |
| 6. 125 | 14. 131 | 22. 133 |
| 7. 117 | 15. 130 | 23. 133 |
| 8. 122 | 16. 127 | 24. 127 |

*Comments:* This is the anaerobic threshold (or A.T.) part of the workout. Felt good. Pushed myself at a speed probably just below race pace.

# COOL-DOWN

*Time:* 14:00
*Percentage of total run:* 20
*Action:* Deceleration
*Percentage of MHR:* 70 to 75
*Perceived exertion:* Somewhat hard
*Pulse readings:*

| | |
|---|---|
| 1. 111 | 8. 107 |
| 2. 106 | 9. 112 |
| 3. 106 | 10. 117 |
| 4. 105 | 11. 111 |
| 5. 104 | 12. 106 |
| 6. 105 | 13. 108 |
| 7. 104 | 14. 108 |

*Comments:* During the hard portion of my run, I had been chasing another runner ahead of me on the beach. His presence motivated me to keep moving. When I finally caught him, I used this as an excuse to slow down and run easy.

This workout could be considered the classic A.T. run: an easy warm-up for about 20 percent of the total workout, a gradual acceleration for an equal time period, the A.T. portion for about 40 percent of the total, and a steady cool-down for the final 20 percent of the total time, which was just over 1 hour.

The total time at top speed (the A.T. segment) was 24 minutes, approximately midway between the length of time it would take me to run a 5-K and a 10-K. During that fast portion of the run, my heart rate was between 80 and 90 percent of my MHR. It's a pattern that any runner attempting this type of workout can duplicate with or without a heart monitor.

Experienced runners usually can tell how well they're running by perceived exertion—how they feel, "listening to their bodies." Another way to measure effort, of course, is by running over a measured course. Above the beach is Lake Shore Drive, site of the annual Michigan City Run. I know all the mile marks along that road and could easily catch splits on a memory watch that records that data. Since my 10-K race pace is just under 6 minutes, I would

## RUNNING LIKE THE WIND

Here are seven tips for boosting your power with anaerobic threshold (A.T.) running.

**1.** *Structure your A.T. runs according to experience, not formulas.* Formulas suggested here and elsewhere can offer only broad guidelines. Begin by taking a period of time to warm up, and at the end of your workout, take a nearly equal period to cool down. In between is the heart of your workout, which probably should vary somewhere between 20 and 40 minutes.

**2.** *Run a pace that is comfortably hard.* Dr. Jack Daniels and others recommend a pace that is 15 seconds per mile slower than your best 10-K time. Since my most recent times for that distance have been in the 36-minute range, I would run just slower than 6-minute miles.

**3.** *Run solo.* Unless you have an identical twin, you may have difficulty finding another runner whose anaerobic threshold matches yours. Even when you can (such as in team situations with runners of nearly equal ability), you should be cautious and try to run according to *your* ability. With others, it's too easy to become competitive and push the pace too hard, even in noncompetitive situations.

**4.** *Don't measure your level of intensity by time.* It's too easy to fool yourself into thinking you're improving because you did this week's wind run faster than

need only to run just over 6 minutes to achieve approximately the same results.

I say "approximately" because external factors can render time measurements inaccurate. Hot weather, cold weather, wind, hills, surface conditions—all can make a mile run at a 6-minute pace equal to a 5:30 effort. The fact that I raced a 10-K only two days before probably made my pace on the beach slower than my normal A.T. run. But it didn't matter, last week's. The overload principle works with some forms of training, but not here. It's too easy to cheat by running the warm-up and cool-down sections progressively faster, which defeats the purpose of the workout. By jogging easily at both the beginning and end of each wind run, I eliminate any danger of comparing one workout to another.

**5.** *Run an A.T. run anywhere.* The road. The track. The woods. Even on a treadmill in your basement. The important factor is intensity, not how (or where) that intensity is achieved.

**6.** *Maintain a steady effort, not a steady speed.* If you run out with the wind at your back, then return into the wind. Your actual pace may drop, but not your effort. The same is true on hilly courses, where your pulse actually may rise or drop, depending whether you are going uphill or downhill.

**7.** *Concentrate.* You'll find you are able to run more effectively if you focus on what you are doing rather than allow your mind to drift, as is common among runners on more purely aerobic runs. Because of the speed at which you will be moving, A.T. runs offer a good opportunity to pay attention to how you can maintain good running form. This body awareness will help you improve your racing later.

since I was measuring heart rate and my own perceptions of effort, not time.

## MAXIMUM GAIN FOR MINIMUM DAMAGE

What are the benefits of A.T. training? You get maximum gain for minimum damage. According to Dr. Daniels:

"Threshold-pace training is individualized and adaptable to changes in fitness. It won't cause you to overtrain. It will build your confidence with each workout. And it will produce results, whether you're at the back of the pack, in the middle, or way up front."

How does this training pace compare with race pace? In an article on 10-K training in *Running Research News,* Dr. Owen Anderson identified 5-K runners as racing at 95 to 100 percent of MHR, 10-K runners at 90 to 92 percent of MHR, 15-K and 10-mile runners at 86 percent of MHR, and marathoners at 80 percent of MHR.

Dr. Anderson further suggested that interval training (an intense workout I covered in chapter 8) occurs at 90 to 100 percent of MHR. Dr. Anderson thus concluded that a good pace for A.T. training might be a pace just a bit slower—about 10 to 15 seconds slower per mile—than 10-K pace.

Dr. Daniels, meanwhile, defines A.T. training as a steady, controlled tempo run that lasts about 20 minutes at threshold pace. He considers a steady intensity of effort important. "Going too fast is no better than going too slow," he says. "A tempo run is hard but *controlled.* What's important is the intensity, not the time or speed, which can vary depending on the course, the environment, and whether or not the runner is fatigued or well rested."

One important bonus of such running, according to Dr. Daniels, is that it helps improve the runner's ability to concentrate. You don't float along between 80 and 90 percent of your MHR—at least for any appreciable distance—without being well focused on what you're doing.

Dr. Daniels's recommendation for structuring the workout doesn't differ too much from my beach run: 20 percent of the total time spent in warm-up, 70 percent of the time (20 to 30 minutes) featuring good hard running, and 10 percent of the total time for cool-down.

Dr. Costill, however, warns that A.T. running is not the be-all and end-all of training for all runners. "All it is," he says, "is a semiquantitative way to have somebody run at a point where they are at a high level of aerobic training."

Regardless of what you call it, I find wind running an enjoyable and effective way to run.

Chapter *12*

# POWER HILLS

## BUILD YOUR STRENGTH ON THE WAY TO THE TOP

**T**he University of Oregon's Bill Bowerman was known for his bluntness. I once quizzed him about whether training on hills could make you a better runner. "When they start putting hills on tracks," he replied gruffly, "I'll have my athletes run hills in practice."

It was a classic remark from a classic coach. Yet Arthur Lydiard, the New Zealander whom Bowerman admitted using as a source for many training ideas, strongly recommended hill training for those wanting to improve their speed on track or road. Dean Brittenham of the National Institute for Fitness and Sport also believes that one way runners get stronger (thus faster) is to run up an incline. "Most good training programs have one common philosophy—some type of resistance running," he says. "And the best way to achieve that is with hills."

I live just over the crest of a hill that rises 75 feet above the shores of Lake Michigan. The road in front of my house, Lake Shore Drive, is relatively flat to the west, sloping slightly downward. To the east, however, the road dips more precipitously, losing most of its above-lake altitude within several hundred yards before starting to level off. So right out my front door, I have a nearly ¼-mile hill that's perfect for resistance training.

When I run east, I must begin downhill, which can be painful on days when I am tight from the previous day's hard workout. Returning, I must cope with this hill in the closing minute of my run.

The "Higdon Hill" is a pivotal part of the 15-K course used for the Michigan City Run, a major local race held each June. Runners head down the hill midway through the fourth mile, make a U-turn farther down the road, and come back up it just before the 6-mile mark. The hill therefore becomes the break point where many races are either won or lost. When Bill Rodgers ran Michigan City in 1978, I pointed out to him that the hill (which, because of a bend in the road, seems to go on forever) steepens just before the crest, but once over the top, he could use the quick drop and the gentle decline that follows over the next ½ mile to gain momentum for a long surge to the finish. And that's where Rodgers left the other competitors in the race.

# LEARNING TO LOVE HILLS

Let's talk about hills. Uphills and downhills. Big hills and small hills. Hills as both aid and deterrent to performance. Hills in training and hills in races. Hills as both a cause and a preventive of injuries. How to run them and how to avoid them; what to do when you don't have them, yet you still have to race on a hilly course. Hills to build strength and hills to build speed. Hills to build courage and hills to discourage. Are they an essential training tool or a gimmick dreamed up by a New Zealand coach out to prove to joggers that they'll never make it as serious racers?

The coach is Arthur Lydiard, who has outlined hill running in his books and numerous lectures as an essential ingredient of his three-step training buildup, which includes:

1. Endurance training
2. Hill training
3. Speedwork

Lydiard didn't discover hill training, however, any more than Zebulon Montgomery Pike discovered the mountain bearing his name. The Indians arrived at the peak before Pike, and Percy Cerutty was using hills before Lydiard to train Australian athletes such as Herb Elliott, 1500-meter champion at the 1960 Olympics. Cerutty used to send Elliott sprinting up sand dunes near his training center at Portsea. Even before Cerutty, there were other coaches and runners who advocated hill running to build stamina, although Cerutty may have been the only coach to claim that running at full pace up a hill could bring "relief from constipation."

Lydiard made no such claims. He was less a discoverer of hill training than one who developed a systemized program. Lydiard's athletes, including Olympic champions Murray Halberg and Peter Snell, did not merely run hills, they trained on them at specific points in their season to peak for specific races.

Lydiard's hill workouts had a pattern. His athletes would run a 5-mile warmup, then run up a ½-mile hill, run ¼ mile fast on top, run hard downhill, and run ¼ mile of quick fartlek at the bottom. They'd do six or eight of these hill loops, followed by a 2-mile cool-down. This was hardly the sort of workout schedule you would suggest to a beginner, but after Lydiard's runners started to win at the Olympics, track fans began to ask, what is it that they are doing differently? It was running hills.

Although Lydiard's endorsement was unequivocal, the

research is inconclusive. Studies related to the specificity of exercise suggest that if you plan to race on hills, you need to train on hills. But whether such training also makes you a better runner on the flat, and on the track, is difficult to measure in the laboratory. (Apparently, Bowerman's reasoning for not recommending hill training to track athletes was well founded.) But Lydiard believes that running up and down hills can make you a faster runner — and the achievements of his athletes would seem to support him.

# THE ADVOCATES AND THE SKEPTICS

Physiologist Dr. Jack Daniels's research at the Nike Sport Research Laboratory in Exeter, New Hampshire, determined that the addition of hill running does indeed increase the intensity of a training program. A runner's energy cost, he found, increases 12 percent when running up a 1-degree slope, but only 7 percent of the energy returns when coming down that same slope.

Yet Jack H. Wilmore, Ph.D., supervised a project by graduate students Doug Allen and Beau Freund while at the University of Arizona. They trained two groups of runners, one on the flat, the other running a gradual stadium ramp. At the end of the study, they found no difference between the two groups, at least not in the changes of their $VO_2$ max. "That tells you something," says Dr. Wilmore, "although maybe athletes don't want to hear it." (Dr. Wilmore and his team did not measure performance by testing the runners on a track or in races, so it *is* possible that hill training might have some important mental benefits, convincing runners they are tougher.)

Ball State researcher Dr. David Costill maintains that theoretically, hill training should improve speed. "In order to have good speed," he says, "you must create force through the thigh and hamstring muscles, and hill work develops both." But Dr. Costill has not researched the subject and knows of no other exercise physiologists who have.

"Hill training is another form of resistance," claims Dr. Ned Frederick of the Nike Sport Research Laboratory. "All training boils down to cleverly increasing the amount of resistance that your body can adapt to. So running uphill is one way of tricking the body. But there is no magic to hill training, no special adaptation that you can't get somewhere else."

Bob Glover, co-author of *The Runner's Handbook,* believes that if you plan to race on hills, you need to train on hills. He offers several reasons, however, why even runners racing on flat courses should consider training on hills.

- Uphill intervals can be used to improve your form. You must concentrate on form to get up the hill.
- Downhill runs can teach relaxation and improve leg speed and stride.
- Hill running is "speedwork in disguise." It can be used in place of grueling track workouts to improve your anaerobic efficiency.
- Hills strengthen your legs, especially the quads, lessening the possibility of knee injury.
- Your mental ability to handle hills in races improves. Glover adds: "If you live in the flatlands, be creative. Highway ramps or parking garages are possibilities, although they may pose obvious safety problems."

# ELITE ADVICE ON HILLS

Whether to build strength or to condition themselves for hilly races, most top runners use hills in their training. Bill Rodgers, who has an excellent reputation as a hill runner (particularly on the descent), is among them. He once told me: "First, as an uphill runner, I'm weak. I've tried to do more hill repeats to compensate for this. Downhill, my success may be just from the way I land, my lightness. But even in high school, my coach emphasized pushing *over* the hill and not running as hard going up.

"I don't practice downhill running. The only time I would run hills was before Boston. I started to do more uphill training when I saw how well Randy Thomas and Greg Meyer ran on the uphills."

Rodgers used to train on none other than Heartbreak Hill, the fourth of the Newton hills that comes near the 21-mile mark on the course of the Boston Marathon, which he won four times. Although Heartbreak Hill is not particularly steep, it is about 600 yards long. Rodgers would run on the grass parkway beside the road, doing six to ten repeats in 1:35. Between uphill bursts, he would jog back down, letting the grass cushion the impact of the downhill (an important step in injury prevention). "I see a lot of other runners training on Heartbreak," says Rodgers, "particularly before Boston."

When Joan Benoit Samuelson coached at Boston University, she often took her team there. "The girls on the team enjoyed it," recalls Samuelson. They would do five to eight repeats. Other times, they ran Summit Avenue Hill, several miles from Heartbreak but not on the marathon course. Samuelson notes that it usually took her team two or three days to recover after a workout on Summit.

"Living in Boston back then, I didn't get onto hills that often," she commented on the training that led her to an Olympic marathon victory in 1984. "During the course of a run, if I came to a hill, I would really charge it." Now living in Maine, Samuelson has more access to hilly running areas.

Herb Lindsay, formerly a number one–ranked road runner, lives in Boulder, Colorado, where the Flatiron Mountains provide "hills" that rise several thousand feet above the city. Canyons feature numerous trails for training. Lindsay feels that the rolling plains before the front range also offer an opportunity for specific hill training, although he prefers the term *incline training*.

"At altitude, one of the negative factors is that you can't get the quality of speed training you can at sea level," Lindsay explains. "You're limited by the thin air, but you can compensate by running on a gentle downhill incline. With gravity pushing you along, you can run as fast (that is, with the same leg speed) as you can at sea level. I do train on uphills, but I probably use downhills with more planning."

## WHAT TO DO WHEN THERE ARE NO HILLS

One strong believer in hill training is former American 5000-meter record holder Marty Liquori, which may seem strange when you consider where Liquori lives: Gainesville, Florida, which is as flat as one of coach Bowerman's tracks. As a substitute for hills, Liquori ran the stadium steps at the University of Florida. He says: "My feeling is that if Arthur Lydiard had a stadium in Auckland like we have in Gainesville, he would promote stadium running. Florida's stadium seats 70,000 people and has three levels of incline that get progressively steeper; it takes 35 seconds to reach the top, and nobody can run up it more than about eight times."

Liquori would train there once or twice a week before the track season. In between "uphills," he sometimes would run an easy 4 × 400 on the track to loosen up, then go back up the stadium. "At the end, you're totally rigged," he recalls.

Liquori's "stadiums" can be compared with Lydiard's ½-mile hills, coming as they did during a specific segment of his training year. Liquori ran the stadium in a transition period between distance running and track work. "When you run a lot of distance, your stride shortens," says Liquori. "Your leg muscles are not extending, so they become fairly weak. You go to a hill phase to make a transition, to force you to open up your stride by bounding up hills. You exaggerate knee lift and arm swing, push off with the toes and calves. This strengthens your quadriceps and buttocks muscles before going back onto the track. It's right out of the Lydiard book."

Another important factor, believes Liquori, is that somebody who has limited time for training can fatigue the muscles more rapidly on hills than on the flat. "When I was traveling and knew I had only a half hour to work out," he says, "I'd look for a hill. I could get more exhausted than doing a 90-minute run."

In a situation where you have neither mountains nor a stadium nearby, yet you face scheduled races on hilly courses, you may need to try another training modification. Fred Wilt says: "If you are not going to run uphill in training, you have to do a lot of running where you go at one pace, then cut loose for 50 yards. The energy requirements for going uphill are so much greater than on the flat, you have to get used to higher energy expenditures in a race."

## USING HILLS TO BUILD MUSCLE

Jeff Galloway wrote in an article in *Runner's World:* "Many coaches and strength experts believe hills provide better strength for running than weights or machines. Pushing up the incline builds the lower leg muscles. With power there, you can develop a more efficient push-off, better running posture, and more strength in your legs.

"Weight lifting strengthens those same muscles, but it won't train them for the demands of running. The large and small muscles in the legs must work together perfectly to produce a smooth stride. Hill running builds strength and coordination at the same time."

Ron Gunn, track coach at Southwestern Michigan College, often uses a 200-meter sloping fairway on a golf course near campus. There he has his team do circuit sprinting on the grass following a fast run of 5 to 7 miles. He calls the circuit "Scando-loops" after the Scandinavians. Here's how Gunn defines the workout: "Go at a faster-than-race pace up the hill, then do a relaxing jog around the top. Run easily the first 75 meters of the downhill that is steep; then when the drop begins to level out, relax and lift up on the balls of the feet, arms vertical, and sprint down the hill. It's what we call 'going into fifth gear.' Get back down to the bottom, then jog some more, sprint again at the bottom, jog some more, go up again. Do about six of those. It develops speed and strength, and it also teaches you to run a hill properly."

Another Gunn hill circuit utilizes an old country road featuring a hill with three levels, where his runners alternate fast and slow running according to the pitch of the hill. Gunn has his squad do hill training twice a week for as many as eight weeks prior to a major competition. Sometimes the hills serve as just one part of a structured program, other times they make up the entire workout. He says: "Hills also are good for getting into condition quickly without the risk of injury. You don't have to do a lot of running to obtain a quality workout. You don't need as many repetitions."

Liquori adds: "With the caliber of runners we have today, they can't get tired doing interval work on a track. You could take a workout like 20 quarters in 55 seconds, and today's runners just might be able to do it. But before they finish, an Achilles tendon would flare up, or ligaments would give way. Running hills permits you to do more by doing less. When you get to the point where everybody runs 120 miles a week at a 5:30 pace, you have to find other ways to generate more stress. Hills may be the wave of the future."

## PUTTING HILLS
## INTO YOUR WORKOUT

Obviously, elite runners turn to hills to add an intensity to their workouts they just can't get anywhere else. But what about the runners who inhabit the middle of the pack? Gunn can tell you. He has coached just such people in classes at his community college: men and women, young and old, with little background as competitive athletes. "They do circuits on the same hills," says Gunn, "only involving different techniques. As with our college students, I'll have them do some kind of tempo run; then they'll end up in the latter stage of the workout doing hills. They'll start with three to four and build up to seven or eight, running faster than race pace, then turn around and jog down. They won't do the other phases.

"We run on golf courses or forest trails. We've gotten off hard roads now. It's pretty difficult to injure an athlete running up a hill. The time you have to be careful is coming down."

At the Nike Sport Research Laboratory, Tom Clark studied the impact shock of running up and down hills. Ten well-trained runners ran at various grades, from 6 percent uphill to 8 percent downhill, at a 7-minute-mile pace. At the steepest uphill grade, the shock was only 85 percent of that experienced running on level ground. The steepest downhill grade resulted in 40 percent *more* leg shock—an increased risk of injury.

It may be, then, that hill training—particularly intensive training—and running fast downhill should be reserved for days when you are well rested and at a point during your workout where you are relaxed from a good warm-up but not yet excessively fatigued. "You're more likely to injure yourself when you're tired," says Herb Lindsay of his incline training.

Of course, what goes up must come down—or does it? Marty Liquori claimed one trick he learned from New Zealanders Rod Dixon and John Walker was to not run downhill. Liquori explains: "Instead of 4-minute intervals on a track, they would go 10 minutes up a steep hill and get a ride back down." That suggests the ultimate athletic perk—a satisfied coach standing beside a limousine at the top of a mountain. Even without that, most runners who attempt hill training will find that it makes them better runners.

## THERE'S GOLD IN THOSE HILLS

Once you agree that training on hills can make you a faster runner, you should also be ready to develop a hill-running technique. One summer, I taught at the Green Mountain Running Camp in northern Vermont. Each morning from our hilltop campus at Lyndon State College, I looked out over a rolling landscape. Fog settled in the valleys; hills above touched the sky. I wanted to run those hills forever.

But as I discovered from observing the runners at the camp, not everybody knows how to run hills—up or down. Their main form fault was not knowing how to lean. They leaned into the hill going up; they leaned backward going down. Actually, they should have been doing the opposite.

# HOW TO MAKE
## UPHILL RUNNING A BREEZE

Here are five tips that will make running uphill easier and more comfortable. Use them the next time you face a tall hill. They will surely give you an edge in both your racing and your training.

**1.** *Enjoy the hill.* Consider the hill an opportunity to relax, change pace, and use different muscles.

**2.** *Look upward.* This helps you keep your body angle perpendicular to the ground, best for traction.

**3.** *Shift gears.* Seek a short, quick stride. You want the most efficient tempo for least wasted energy.

**4.** *Don't push.* Hills are hard only if you make them hard. You need not maintain your same speed from the flats.

**5.** *Run over the top.* Cresting the hill, quickly resume your previous pace from the flat. A cyclist would shift to high here; a skier would pole off. So should you.

## THE DOS AND DON'TS
## OF UPHILL RUNNING

Let's focus first on uphills, which trouble runners most. Runners can learn about hill-running technique from skiers and cyclists. Going uphill, a cross-country skier looks toward the top of the slope. Raising his gaze causes a slight shift backward in weight, anchoring each ski plant enough to avoid slipping. If he leans forward, his skis lose traction. At the end of cross-country ski races, I constantly have to fight the tendency to slump forward from fatigue, which causes my skis to slide backward.

The same is true in cycling. My first time on a mountain bike, I also learned quickly to sit back in the saddle going up the trail. When I did otherwise, my wheels spun. For best bike traction, you keep weight over the power (rear) wheel. The same is true for running: Learn to lean back when going uphill.

Also change your tempo when starting uphill. Just as a cyclist downshifts for more power, runners need to change gears by shortening and quickening stride. But don't push too hard uphill; otherwise, you won't have enough stamina to run fast downhill.

## SKILLS FOR RUNNING DOWNHILL

Running downhill takes another skill and a different attitude. In the closing miles of the Boston Marathon, people lining Commonwealth Avenue encourage runners by shouting: "It's downhill all the way!" Actually, most runners find it more difficult running down than up. Uphill, you can survive on guts; downhill requires skill and practiced techniques.

I learned about downhill running from Kenny Moore, the 1968 and 1972 Olympic marathoner who writes for *Sports Illustrated*. During the course of researching hill running for a two-part article that appeared in *Runner's World*, I was told by several runners that Moore was their downhill running guru. I contacted him and later received a letter that, even nearly two decades later, is probably worth reprinting in full.

I have a recurring dream (it has come twice) in which I plunge blithely over a cliff and run down the face with floating, 60-foot strides. But instead of coming to an abrupt flattening, it happens that the incline gradually becomes less severe. My gravity-assisted bounds shorten to 50, then 40, feet. My speed drops from 125 mph to 80. Eventually, assuming my hamstrings stay relaxed as the hillside rips my feet along under my torso at a rate six times as fast as my muscles can do it by themselves, I emerge safely on the level plain, a couple of miles beneath my starting point, where I ultimately starve to death.

I don't suppose it is possible. But it might serve as illustration of the sort of things which facilitate downhill running.

Primary, I think, is raw smugness, preferably born of experience, which will let one bolt freewheeling down a slope without any fear of falling. That fear, I'm sure, works against the kind of relaxation necessary. It takes, at first anyway, a bit of nerve to lean forward so the torso is perpendicular to the surface of the hill, and to run with the same action and footplant one would use on the level. The idea, of course, is to let gravity do all the work, and that can't happen if you're clunking down on your heels or shooting the soles of your feet along the pavement.

Downhill running takes practice as well, to condition the thighs to the intense pounding. And to get the legs used to the much higher rates of stride, even if the backs of the legs and back don't have to do anything but follow along. I find downhill strides wonderful speed training, but that's nothing new. Lydiard has taught it in New Zealand for years, and in 1960, Alan Lawrence ran intervals (440s in 48.0, 660s in 1:14, if I remember correctly) hanging on to the back of a car. He thought it helped him and stressed the need for confidence. I'm sure it was the same sort of thing.

The only other tip I can offer: Don't reach the top of a hill exhausted, or it won't work. I'll give up 5 or 10 yards uphill to anyone and get twice that down the other side if I'm able to save enough energy to keep my knees up.

The main problem in downhill running, as Moore clearly understood, is attitude. Not mental attitude, but the way the astronauts use that term to describe positioning a space capsule. When I interviewed Mario Andretti for a book I was writing about auto racing, he also talked about attitude when it came to angling his race car into a turn at the Indy 500.

The right attitude for downhill runners is leaning forward. Just as you can learn from skiers and cyclists going uphill by leaning backward and shifting gears, you also can learn from these other athletes on the downs.

Going downhill, a skier keeps weight evenly distributed on his skis but tilts forward from the waist into a tuck position to minimize wind drag. The same with a cyclist. Runners need not worry as much about drag, but they also should tilt forward to let the hill carry them down. Not only will you go faster, but you minimize pounding by getting off your heels. Braking slows you and wastes the effort you just invested in running uphill.

Here's where attitude comes in, because you want to *tilt*

## HOW TO USE FREE SPEED
## ON THE DOWNHILL

You *will* go faster when you run downhill. It's free speed. But that's not always a welcome sensation if the hill is too steep. Here is a four-step method to cope with this increasing speed.

**1.** Starting downhill, tilt forward, beginning at the waist. How much you tilt depends on the angle of the hill.

**2.** As you move faster, raise your knees and lengthen your stride to cope with the increased speed.

**3.** For better balance, particularly on uneven ground, allow your elbows to rise up and out.

**4.** To cushion the shock of the descent, land more on the front of your foot rather than on your heels.

Most important, practice! Like technique in any sport, learning to run downhill takes time. Running downhill becomes more difficult toward the end of a long run or race, when fatigue makes the concentration necessary to perform skills such as those listed above difficult. Those people shouting encouragement at the end of the Boston Marathon mean well, but running downhill is no easier than piloting a spacecraft or driving a race car at Indy.

forward, not merely lean. The tilt begins at the pelvis and is ever so slight. To master this pelvic tilt, you need practice. Find a long downhill—not too steep—and experiment with different tilts as you run, seeing what angle changes do to both your speed and comfort.

Chapter *13*

# STRENGTH TRAINING

## SHAVE YOUR TIME WITH WEIGHTS

**B**ecause I am a believer in preventive medicine, I have physical examinations on a regular basis, usually every other year. My most recent exams have been at the Cooper Clinic in Dallas, founded by Kenneth H. Cooper, M.D., author of the best-selling book *Aerobics*.

Central to the exam is an exercise stress test. After being fitted with electrodes that monitor my heartbeat, I step onto a treadmill, which begins moving at a relentless 3.3 mph. Each minute it tilts 1 degree, to a maximum of 25 degrees in 25 minutes. By that point, what started as an easy walk has become a difficult uphill run. Most people tested by Dr. Cooper don't make it to 25 minutes—a very high level of physical fitness.

Even if you do last the full 25 minutes, the intensity builds and builds. Running up a 25-degree incline, it's very difficult to face the speed increases of 0.2 mph per minute. It doesn't take long before you're ready to cry halt. It's the standard Balke Protocol, which is used by many physicians and researchers. Toward the end of the test, Dr. Cooper usually appears—ostensibly to serve as cheerleader, but also to be present in case of any problems.

On my last visit to Dallas, I reached 30 minutes before leg fatigue forced me to stop. That placed me not only near the top of my age group, Dr. Cooper informed me, but in the "superior" cardiovascular fitness classification for men of *any* age. When it comes to running on a treadmill, I'm right up there in the 99th percentile.

This is pretty heady stuff. Then I headed for the physical therapy laboratory, where I proceeded to flunk my strength test!

Okay . . . that's not entirely true, since I at least do sit-ups reasonably well. But my knee extension and flexion, as measured on a Cybex machine, ranges from poor to average. My leg press and bench press rate me only fair. Even when adjusted for body weight, I rank only average. "In looking at the strength profile," Dr. Cooper wrote in his report, "your overall strength is considerably less than what would be expected in view of your athletic ability." He suggested that I concentrate on a few more exercises to strengthen my back and upper body.

Dr. Cooper, of course, is more interested in total physical fitness than in speed performance. A certain level of strength improves your quality of life, and it may even improve your next 10-K time. But many serious runners ignore, or even avoid, exercises that might strengthen them.

Tom Brunick, a consultant with The Athlete's Foot chain, claims that too many runners look like "vertical hyphens." We're skinny, with no upper-body mass. This is because we prefer to focus our time and energy on the sport we enjoy— running. We don't want to waste time pumping iron. But in making this choice, we may be ignoring a supplemental discipline that could help us to run fast.

# WEIGHING YOUR ADVANTAGE

Some runners find that weight lifting or other forms of strength training do make a difference. Still, researchers contend that there is no conclusive evidence. It depends partly on your running event, partly on your ability, partly on how much you run. Most scientists concede that documented studies fail to demonstrate any benefit of weight lifting for young, male, elite runners—although they may for individuals in other categories. Studies at the University of Massachusetts in Amherst, for example, have shown strength gains of 10 to 15 percent among older runners who add weight training to their schedules. But Daniel Becque, Ph.D., who conducted the study, admits strength may be more important for sprinters than for distance runners. "For Gelindo Bordin [Olympic and Boston Marathon champion] to suddenly start pumping iron would be fruitless," says Dr. Becque.

I've discussed the subject on several occasions with Ball State's Dr. David Costill. He claims that strength training makes you a better weight lifter, but not necessarily a better runner. "There's no raw, objective data," he says, "that proves you will run faster if you weight train."

## LEARNING ABOUT STRENGTH FROM THE EXPERTS

Still, weight training has its share of running advocates. Lawrence E. Armstrong, Ph.D., a former colleague of Dr. Costill's, believes that power training can help improve your stride length—one element that separates fast runners from slow ones. Dr. Armstrong currently is with the Department of Sport, Leisure, and Exercise Sciences at the University of Connecticut. He did his graduate work at Ball State, where he collaborated with Dr. Costill on a study that attempted to measure the difference between sprinters and distance runners.

The sprinters were more muscular; the distance runners

were more lean. Dr. Costill and Dr. Armstrong filmed the athletes during a maximum sprint. They noted that at maximum speed, the sprinters and distance runners had identical body angles: straight up. But they also found a revealing difference—stride lengths. At maximum velocity, the sprinters' stride lengths were longer than the distance runners', although stride frequencies were the same. Apparently, a longer stride is what permitted the sprinters to run faster for shorter distances. It gave them a special "kick."

"Because stride length, and not stride frequency, is paramount to speed production," Dr. Armstrong summarized in his report, "training should focus on the muscles which produce a long, powerful stride, namely the muscles of the hip, thigh, and lower leg." He noted that speedwork develops those muscles. He felt that the study supported those coaches who recommend power drills, such as uphill training and bounding, to improve leg strength, which consequently lengthens the stride. But he also suggested that weight lifting might add an "extra edge" and help to stabilize joints by strengthening the surrounding musculature.

To increase the power output of the hip flexors, hip extensors, knee extensors, and ankle extensors, Dr. Armstrong recommends half squats, leg lunges, hip extensions, and heel raises. He warns that the transition to power training should be gradual to avoid ligament, muscle, or tendon damage.

**Half squats:** Stand with your feet shoulder width apart (or wider), with the weight of the barbell resting across the shoulders and behind the neck. Bend your knees and lower your body until the tops of your thighs are parallel to the floor. Dr. Armstrong recommends that the descent be constant, slow, and controlled. The barbell should remain stable—that is, with very little movement forward or rearward. After reaching the bottom position, begin your ascent, keeping the movement constant but rapid. Complete the movement with a forward hip roll. This exercise strenghtens four muscles: the quadriceps, hamstrings, gluteals, and erector spinae.

**Leg lunges:** Start this exercise in the same position as the half squats. Take a long step forward with one leg and descend to a low position, then rise. Bring the lead leg back and repeat with the other leg forward. This exercise strengthens the same four muscles as the half squats.

**Heel raises:** Again, stand with your feet shoulder width apart, the barbell resting on your shoulders behind your neck. Use a support block ½ to 1 inch high. Stand with the balls of your feet on the block and your heels on the ground, but otherwise in the same position as for the first two exercises. Raise your heels off the ground so that all the weight is forward, on your toes. Your movement should be deliberate and controlled. Return to the starting position and repeat. This exercise strengthens the gastroc nemius and soleus, the main muscles of the lower leg.

**Hip extensions:** This exercise is best performed using an exercise machine that features cables and pulleys, with a brace on the end of the cable in which you can position your calf. Stand straight, facing the wall or the machine, and hold onto the machine for support. Your legs should be shoulder width apart. Move the braced leg back to a 45-degree angle. Bend your support leg if necessary, but your braced leg should remain straight. Return your leg against resistance to the starting position and repeat. Switch legs. With the exception of the quadriceps, this exercise strengthens the same muscles as half squats.

These exercises surely will improve your leg power and maybe will make you a better sprinter. But would they make you a better distance runner?

The same question troubled me. Concerned by my poor strength performance at the Cooper Clinic, I returned home and consulted Charles Wolf, director of the physical therapy department at Memorial Hospital in Michigan City. Dr. Cooper's test showed I had little power for the leg and knee extensions, even for my age group. But he was measuring pure *power,* the kind the makes you a better sprinter or weight lifter. Wolf duplicated the tests but added one more—a leg endurance test that involved 30 repetitions rather than just four, as used in Dr. Cooper's test. On the 30th rep, I was kicking with almost the same power as on the first. I had endurance.

But what about strength? "As a distance runner, you don't need a lot of strength," said Wolf. "You just need a little strength at the right time." The "right time" is the moment that the leg pushes off of the ground, propelling the runner forward. That particular action is a *functional* strength, and it's best trained by running. For distance runners, therefore, weight training can only be a supplemental activity.

## THREE RUNNERS WHO BENEFIT MOST

Do you think *your* running would benefit from weight training? Certain individuals probably benefit more from strength training than others.

**Ectomorphs:** These are individuals considered to be of the slender physical type—"having a thin body build," my dictionary politely says—the ones Brunick describes as "vertical hyphens." Ectomorph is the opposite of endomorph, someone with more muscle and a heavier body build. You know who you are, you ectomorphs. I'm one of you. I'm effective as a runner because I weigh only 142 pounds. The most muscular part of my body is my legs. The front ranks of any distance race consist primarily of ectomorphs, who, as kids, were among the last picked for neighborhood football games. (The sport of 10-K racing might be called The Revenge of the Skinnies!) Many, if not most, of these front-runners probably need to do at least some weight lifting to maintain their strength and speed—as long as they can do it without significantly increasing their bulk or weight.

**Women:** One of the main differences between men and women is strength. It's a simple fact of genetics. Exercise scientists frequently cite this strength difference to explain why female athletes in all sports—golf, tennis, skiing—cannot compete on equal terms with their male counterparts. Thus, women probably can benefit more from strength training than men—as long as the extra strength does not equal extra weight.

**Masters:** "Strength fades as we age," insists the University of Florida's Dr. Michael L. Pollock. "As strength fades, so does speed." It's easily measurable in the laboratory. As we move through the ages, from 30 to 40 to 50 and onward, we lose strength faster than endurance. That's one reason why older runners have more success in ultramarathons than in 1500-meter races against younger runners. "As you get older, you need to focus more and more on this [strength] aspect of your conditioning," says Dr. Pollock.

George Lesmes, Ph.D., director of the Human Performance Laboratory at Northeastern Illinois University, notes that he has been able to increase the endurance of men 55 and over by offering them strength training for their legs. "They can stay up on the treadmill longer," says Dr. Lesmes, "and it's simply a matter of strength equaling improved endurance."

Given the above, the person most likely to improve running speed through strength training would be a female masters runner with a slight build.

Does that mean that if you are a muscular young male, you need not worry about strength training? More than likely, the benefits for you will be less, but the effects of weight training *are* noticeable in race conditions.

# TRAINING FOR PERFORMANCE

The rules are set: Muscle fiber cannot be *created*. Genetics determines how many muscles we have. Muscle fibers, however, can be *thickened,* an increase in size that is called hypertrophy. Dean Brittenham of the National Institute for Fitness and Sport explains that lifting heavy loads (more weight, fewer repetitions) tends to build maximum strength and muscle size. Lifting less weight but with more repetitions develops greater muscle endurance, along with muscle definition.

But competitive runners are not interested in muscle size or muscle definition, the pumped-up look that you see on bodybuilders. Until Schwarzenegger shows that he is as adept at running fast 10-Ks as he is at making box-office hits, most runners will decline to follow his type of training.

Yet maybe we should give strength a chance. When Gabriel Mirkin, M.D., once wrote in *The Runner,* "There is no proof that [lifting] will in any way improve your times," a reader from New Jersey replied in strong disagreement. "Dr. Mirkin may be correct for runners blessed with a fair amount of upper-body strength," he wrote. "But I had very little strength to begin with and have found (after 6 months of Nautilus training) that I can now run any race without the extreme fatigue I formerly felt in my shoulders and arms."

Good point, but that proves only that strength training benefited that particular runner. It may not benefit all of us. So how do you know if weight training is right for you? Let's consider the subject further.

## *FIGHTING UPPER-BODY FATIGUE*

Masters runner Bob Schlau is one who believes that strength training can improve speed. He told me about his own experience for an article on strength training I was writing for *Runner's World.* Schlau claimed that prior to 1980, his arms and shoulders always tired toward the end of a race (usually a marathon). His legs also started moving more slowly, so his pace fell off. "My upper body would just go dead," he told me. "I know it affected my times."

Hoping to improve his performances, Schlau began a strength-training program for his upper body. He developed a three-day-a-week routine of weight work that included sit-ups, stretching, and free weights. "All upper-body stuff,"

Schlau said. "Mostly curls and presses. I also take light weights and replicate the running motion with my arms."

Did it work? Soon after starting his strength routine, Schlau found he no longer had trouble with arm and shoulder fatigue. And it improved his 5-K and 10-K times as well. At age 42, he ran a 30:48 10-K. It is the contention of Dr. Becque, of course, that strength training is particularly important for masters like Schlau: "One of the first things you lose as you age is power," he says.

Yet one of the most successful masters runners claims he never weight trains. Norm Green, a minister from Wayne, Pennsylvania, won the 10,000 meters at both the 1987 and 1989 World Veterans Championships. His 10,000 time in the 1989 meet in Eugene, Oregon, at age 57 was a rather incredible 33:00. I say "incredible" because I got a good look at Norm as he lapped me. Green is a naturally powerful, well-muscled runner. Yet he claims he relies only on the basics. He just runs hard in every workout and rarely lets his pace lag slower than 6 minutes per mile.

Would Norm Green benefit from strength training? The evidence suggests that Green runs fast enough without benefit of pumping iron. Has Bob Schlau benefited from strength training? It's possible that his fast 10-K times come from other aspects of his training, but I'm not about to suggest that Schlau walk away from the weight room. And I'm not asking Green to join Schlau. They're individuals. Each benefits from different types of training.

## LIFTING FOR ALL-AROUND FITNESS

To develop an all-around fitness program, Dr. Pollock suggests a minimum of two days a week of resistance training. Each session should last approximately 20 minutes and include 8 to 12 repeats on each of the major muscles of the body: legs, hips, trunk, back, arms, and shoulders. This is in addition to a general aerobic program (such as running) that also should include warm-up, stretching, and cooldown. "It's important to exercise all major muscle areas of the body," says Dr. Pollock. "Aerobics is good for legs and heart and body composition, but it won't strengthen muscles or maintain their strength, so a well-rounded program is very necessary."

Keep in mind that Dr. Pollock is more interested in developing fitness, not speed. Someone hoping to use strength training to run fast might like to try my own routine. Despite Dr. Cooper's report, I have always incorporated weight training into my program. And I find it successful.

# PUTTING FREE WEIGHTS TO WORK

In 1958, I competed in the National AAU 30-K Championships in York, Pennsylvania, and placed third. The main sponsor was the York Barbell Company, whose president, Bob Hoffman, was an avid fitness promoter. My prize was a pair of barbells.

For several years, I used the barbells on my back porch. Untutored, I utilized the three Olympic lifts used in weight-lifting competition: three attempts at each lift to see how much iron I could throw over my head. (Don't even ask!) I also worked out occasionally in the weight room at the University of Chicago. That was rather unusual for a distance runner in those days, but I then considered pumping iron as much a form of play as of serious training.

Eventually, I donated my York barbells to a needy Chicago high school where I coached. I drifted away from weight lifting for a decade, then bought a set of weights for my son. When he went to college, I appropriated them.

In the mid-1970s, I met Bill Reynolds, an Olympic lifting candidate who wrote *The Complete Weight Training Book*. We were both speakers at a clinic in California sponsored by *Runner's World*. Reynolds was cautious about promising benefits for distance runners, but nevertheless, he taught five basic lifts.

**Clean and press:** This is one of the Olympic lifts. Standing with your feet spread about shoulder width, reach down, grasp the bar, and bring it overhead in one continuous movement. Return the bar to the floor and repeat.

**Bent-over rowing:** With your knees slightly bent to relieve stress on your back, reach down and grasp the bar with your palms down. Lift it to your chest without rising from the bent position. Return the bar to the floor and repeat.

**Upright rowing:** Again with your palms down, bring the bar to an upright position, standing straight with the bar resting against the front of your thighs. Letting your elbows go out to the side, raise the bar to chest height, keeping it close to your body, and repeat.

**Curl:** This is a basic lift for any weight-training routine. Assume the same upright position as above, with the bar resting against the front of your thighs. This time, though, your palms should be up instead of down. With your elbows close to your body, lift the bar to chest height and repeat.

**Military press:** Perhaps *the* most basic lift. In the upright position, with your palms down, bring the bar to shoulder height. Raise the bar overhead, fully extending your arms, and repeat.

Following Reynolds's advice, I did these routines with low weights and high repetitions. I stretched between sets of ten and lifted only every other day—usually during the off-season, when I had no important races.

# REAPING BENEFITS FROM MACHINES

My wife, Rose, played tennis at a local health club, so we had a family membership. When the club added a Nautilus center, I moved some of my training there. While Rose was snapping backhands, I pumped iron.

From visits to that tennis club and other fitness centers, I discovered that the first time you appear and ask the attendant (who may or may not know anything about running) what machines to use, he will try to convince you to use all of them, and regularly. That was part of the Nautilus pitch, but I recommend selectivity. Frank Shorter once told me he worked only on his upper body, and I did the same. My favorite was the pullover machine, where I sat on a bench and pulled down a bar from overhead to a position in front of me. I liked it because it did a good job of approximating the double-pole motion essential to good cross-country skiing, a sport in which I was trying to improve.

In addition to the pullover machine, I worked on the torso, arm, rowing, lateral raise, and overhead press machines. Walk into any fitness center, and the attendant can guide you to these machines or to others designed to improve upper-body strength.

Earlier I experimented with leg extensions and leg curls, but I found my knees ached so much the following day that I could hardly run. Lower weights and/or a more gradual buildup might have alleviated that problem, but personally, I feel we strengthen our legs sufficiently by running. At least we strengthen the leg muscles *used* for running, regardless of how we score on various strength tests. Unless you have some specific muscle imbalance, or you have a strength coach who knows something about running supervising your training, I recommend leaving the lower body alone. One distinct advantage of Nautilus and other machine systems is that you can focus on a specific muscle group and avoid stressing others. This is important when suffering from injuries.

## HOME GYM REMEDIES

Eventually, my wife drifted away from tennis, and we canceled our club membership. I purchased a Total Gym for my basement. The Total Gym features a sliding bench that can be adjusted to eight levels, providing eight angles. The greater the angle, the more weight you pull. It is your own weight you're pulling, since you sit or lie on the bench and grasp a pair of grips, attached to the bench by wires that fit through pulleys. Numerous other devices that you pull, including rowing machines, work similarly.

The Total Gym was simply a convenient, low-cost device that seemed to work well for my needs. It was set up for literally dozens of exercises. By process of elimination, I found five routines for my arms and shoulders that seemed to work best.

**The ski:** Lying on my back on the bench, I reach backward as far as I can while holding the pulley grips. I pull the grips forward until they are in position ahead of my hips. Then I relax and slide back to the set position, carefully resisting as I slide. I repeat this motion as many times as I want. I call this exercise the ski, because it mimics the double-pole action in cross-country skiing.

**The swim:** Quickly flipping over, I lie facedown on the bench and pull the grips forward, as in the above exercise. The motion is similar to that used in swimming, thus the name. I used this exercise during a period when I was competing in triathlons. I felt stronger, although that strength never translated into an ability to go very fast in the water.

**The row:** Sitting on the bench facing the pulleys, with my knees up, I mimic a rowing motion. It is similar to the workout you can get on rowing machines.

**The curl:** Sitting on the bench facing forward, I mimic the standard weight-lifting curl. I do this exercise last and sometimes have difficulty equaling the number of reps done during the previous exercises. This is partly because of cumulative fatigue and partly because the biceps used in curls are weaker than the larger shoulder muscles used in the other exercises. I could make this exercise easier by doing it first, but my goal is not to accumulate numbers for a diary. My goal is to strengthen my upper body—no easy task for a vertical hyphen.

**The horizontal squat:** Physical therapist Charles Wolf suggested how I might use the Total Gym to duplicate leg extensions. Lying down with my back on the bench and my legs bent, I put my feet on the bottom grips and push down, straightening my legs in what looks like a horizontal squat.

At the start of my strength-training season, I usually begin at level 2 (out of 8) and eventually move to level 3. I'll begin with 25 reps and progress to a maximum of 100, depending on the bench's angle. Fifty reps of all five exercises at the third level is my most typical workout. I'm not interested in progressing to higher and higher loads to attain maximum strength. I'm mostly interested in developing enough strength to assist me in my fast running and also in maintaining overall physical fitness.

In doing so, I'm simply following Dr. David Costill's advice. He says: "The idea of having a progressive program where you get stronger and stronger may not be the best goal for a runner. Use your weights mainly for a supplemental maintenance program. You don't want to bulk up like a weight lifter. Go through a routine that stresses most of your muscles. Once in a while, push yourself. That should provide enough strength and endurance for most runners."

In my basement, I also have a set of barbells, which I use in connection with the sliding bench. I still use the lifts I learned from Bill Reynolds. Typically I do strength training on "easy" running days, when I have run neither too long nor too fast. Following a run of, say, 5 miles on a wintery day, I return to my basement and partially strip before doing my set of exercises with the sliding bench. After that, I stretch for 5 minutes. I also may include some calisthenics as part of my stretching: sit-ups or push-ups. Finally, I move to the barbell and do one or two of Reynolds's lifts—most often the presses, since they are the most basic lifts. After that, I head for the shower and also spend time soaking in the whirlpool, where I do additional stretching.

On different days when I might run harder, I still may include some strength training, but just a few exercises. And at different times of the year—specifically, during what might be called the serious race season—I eliminate much of this routine. Most often, I abandon lifting during the warm months, but this is a time of year when I am able to add sprints and bounding on the golf course or running in chest-deep water at the beach. Most of my strength training is intuitive; very little is scientific. I do it as much because I enjoy the discipline as from any knowledge that it will improve (or maintain) my speed. I feel extra strength does equal extra speed, but I can't prove it to you. Nevertheless, it's a good enough reason to keep me pumping iron.

# *TIPS FOR THE WEIGHT ROOM*

Here are some pointers to keep in mind before you head for the weight room.

**Running remains your best strength exercise.** Exercise is very specific. To best develop your running muscles, you need to run—and run fast. Hill running is most favored by many runners interested in building strength. Weight lifting and other forms of strength training are important mainly as supplemental activities.

**Don't compete with other lifters.** The worst thing is to walk into a weight room and try to lift the same loads as weight-trained athletes around you. You wouldn't expect a 230-pound hunk to beat you in a 10-K, so don't expect to outperform him in his sport.

**Balance the benefits of free weights vs. machines.** Free weights do a better job of exercising the total body because they stress multiple muscles in a single lift. Machines, on the other hand, isolate muscle groups. If you choose to use free weights, be careful. Since they're not connected to a frame and pulleys, they can be dangerous if you're not accustomed to using them. Dr. Pollock recommends exercise machines for masters because of safety. "As we age, we have balance problems," Dr. Pollock advises. "You're less likely to get hurt using a machine."

**Avoid heavy weights.** If you're interested in improving performance, as opposed to physique, stay away from lifting heavy weights. They may be hard on the lower joints, or they may cause you to bulk up. Excessive upper-body weight is dead weight in a 10-K. Watch your bathroom scale. If your weight-lifting routine causes you to gain bulk, try using less weight with more repetitions.

**Don't try to peak as a weight lifter.** You'll find that strength coaches at health clubs often advise you to fatigue each muscle to its maximum, increasing weights and varying reps as you improve in strength. This is a good system for building muscles and bulk, but as a runner, that is not your goal. Over a period of time, develop a strength workout that you can do comfortably and consistently. Stay with it. Don't feel you need to do more.

**Vary your lifting.** The hard/easy principle works in lifting as well as in running. Lifters typically work one group of muscles one day, then rest those muscles the next day while they exercise a different group. If you're lifting on a daily basis, you may want to do the same.

**Lift on your easy days.** Coming in from a grinding interval workout and heading for the weight room is not a good idea. Save your lifting for those days when you run at an easier pace. Even after your easy run, rest up a bit before hitting the weights. Dean Brittenham suggests doing your strength training at a different time of day from when you run. That way, you'll get more out of each workout.

**Lift most during the off-season.** Not every runner has an off-season, but the best time of year for strength training is when you are not training hard or racing often. For those of us in the North, that's usually in the winter; for those in the hot, sunny South, it may be summer.

**Don't overlook the value of calisthenics.** Sit-ups, push-ups, and pull-ups remain effective means of developing and maintaining strength. You don't need to buy a high-tech machine or join a glitzy health club. You can include calisthenics as part of your regular stretching routine.

**Be your own person.** Eventually, every runner should develop a strength routine specific to his or her own needs. "Whether or not strength training makes you a faster runner," says Dr. Costill, "it makes you a fitter individual."

*Chapter 14*

# THE POLISHING TOUCH

## BE YOUR OWN BEST COACH

ne of the secrets of becoming a faster runner is learning not merely *how* to train but also *when* to train—in other words, putting it all together. In 1988, Lynn Jennings proved herself as one of the world's best runners. Self-coached, she placed sixth at the Olympic Games in Korea—no small accomplishment. But as Jennings herself admitted: "I had stalled out." She wanted to run faster.

"My goal," said Jennings, "wasn't just to be the best American runner; I wanted to be the best in the world." To achieve that goal, she began training in April 1989 under the direction of John Babington, an attorney who coaches for the Liberty Athletic Club in Cambridge, Massachusetts.

The combination clicked. In January 1990, Jennings set

a world indoor record for 5000 meters at the Dartmouth Relays. In February, she broke the American record for the 3000, winning the TAC Track-and-Field Championships. In March, she ran 31:06 for an American road record at the Red Lobster 10-K Classic. And later that month, in Aix-Les-Bains, France, she became the first American woman in 15 years to win the World Cross-Country Championships.

As Jennings already had demonstrated, she knew how to train. She also knew her own physiological strengths and weaknesses, having been tested frequently by expert scientists as a member of Athletics West, the Nike-sponsored club. What Babington offered to Jennings was something that all runners need: organization, an objective look at her abilities, and advice on setting goals and peaking for important contests.

"One thing we did at the outset," recalls Babington, "was that we looked at what was her stable and comfortable level of training. It was a ballpark amount of mileage that involved a carefully chosen intensity. We asked ourselves, what components can we upgrade without exhausting her? What additional training margin could she benefit from?

"There's a general principle that says if you want to get better, don't bite off more than you can chew. All changes should be gradual, not abrupt. Our starting point was based on Lynn's lifestyle and time constraints. We asked ourselves, what one or two things can we change, or upgrade, to make her a better runner?"

Jennings and coach Babington observed that her weekly mileage had been relatively low for a world-class runner, between 50 and 60 miles. They decided to push into the 70s. Jennings benefited from this small shift in her training. "That was one of the main differences between Lynn in 1988 and Lynn in 1990," Babington says.

Training adjustments often are achieved most easily with a coach riding shotgun. The instinct of most runners when they want to improve is to do more, but in some instances, they may be better off doing less. Not every runner is like Jennings, who found she needed to do more to develop an edge. As head of the New York Road Runners Club's coaching program, Bob Glover supervises 20 coaches, who in turn supervise hundreds of runners. "At the beginner level," says Glover, "people benefit from being enrolled in a fitness program, because they tend to do too much too soon. For individuals making the transition into racing, a coach can encourage them. The faster a runner gets, the less there is to push. At the elite level, runners have so much drive they don't need a coach pushing them; they need a coach holding them back."

Coach Jim Huff of Detroit's Motor City Striders stresses the importance of planning: "You need to look at your training program, determine specific goals, and develop a program that will help you accomplish those goals, as long as they are realistic. Unfortunately, a lot of runners don't have the basic know-how to progress toward a goal."

# THE COACH APPROACH

One way you can better plan your training is to obtain a coach—a Babington, Glover, or Huff—who can apply the generally accepted principles of training outlined in this book to your goals. Unfortunately, most runners don't have a coach and never will. I have mostly been self-coached for 25 years. I've found that you don't really need a coach; you need to know coaching principles. Just as there are sound physiological principles involving aerobic and anaerobic training that can help you maximize performance, there also are sound coaching and planning principles that can help you succeed.

Putting together your own coaching program just takes a little planning and the knowledge you've gained from this book. Here are some suggestions that a good coach might offer you.

## PLAN AHEAD

Dr. Edmund Burke once said: "Good order is the foundation of all good things." When coach Babington sought improvement for Jennings, their first action was to sit down and plan her long-range training. I do the same for myself. Flying home from the 1979 World Veterans Championships in Hannover, Germany, I took out paper and pencil and planned my training for the 18 months leading up to the next world meet. That was one reason why I won a gold medal in 1981.

Each year, I review the previous year's results and plan ahead, determining what races to peak for—even determining whether I want to peak. Some years, I focus attention on short track races; other years, I shift to the roads. I may plan for a year off, where I run mainly for fun. But it's a conscious decision. You can't get where you're going without a road map.

## LOOK BEHIND

You also can't get where you're going unless you know where you've been. Record your training on a daily basis. In my office, I have a set of loose-leaf notebooks dating back to 1963, when I was fortunate to have the attention of coach Fred Wilt. He asked me to record daily workouts on 5½ × 8½-inch diary sheets, which he provided. Later, I developed my own diary sheet, which I had printed in large numbers for minimal cost.

I record items such as the date, time, location, surface and conditions, and distance, along with my weight. I also record what I did to warm up and cool down, and any comments concerning the actual run. There's space to record an optional second workout and boxes for race split times. (It's also a good idea to include space to jot down notes on your diet.) I also developed different diary formats for my ski workouts and for my high school team.

Various running diaries can be purchased at book stores. Or you can even record your miles on a simple calendar.

There are several reasons for keeping a diary. One, it provides motivation, the same way reporting your workouts to a coach would be motivational. Two, it allows you to learn from your successes and failures. If you ran well, what type of training was responsible for your success? If you ran poorly or were injured, what training error was responsible?

Running diaries are important equipment, almost as important as running shoes.

## DEFINE YOUR GOAL

What do you want to accomplish with your running? Is it continued fitness and the enjoyment of staying in shape? If so, your training plan will differ from one designed to maximize your performance and to run fast times.

Most runners choose goals that are event-oriented. They desire to run well in a specific event—a local race, a national championship. Event-oriented goals are helpful because they allow you to tie your training to specific dates.

But coach Mary Reed of the Atlanta Track Club warns against choosing too many goals: "A person who wants to simultaneously run a sub-40 10-K and break 3 hours for the marathon is liable to fail at both goals because they are so diverse." Reed suggests concentrating on one or the other to allow more precise planning. "Pick one goal this season, then go after the other the next," she says.

## BE REALISTIC

If your fastest 10-K time after several years of serious training is 35 minutes, you hardly should expect to break 30 minutes and qualify for the Olympic team within a year. Set your goals and plan your training conservatively. If you exceed your hopes, you can always regroup.

Bruce Tulluh, formerly one of Great Britain's fastest 5000-meter runners, writes in *Running:* "When building your own schedule, the first thing to decide is the volume of training which you can handle, both in total and in the number of good sessions a week. The training load you undertake must always be related to what you have been doing, not what you think you ought to do."

## DON'T BE TRAPPED BY HISTORY

Historian Max Lerner once warned that we should learn from history but not be trapped by it. He was thinking of global issues, such as war, but the advice proves apropos for running, too. One of the dangers of having records for several decades of training on your shelves is believing that what once worked may work again. Some of my best training years were 1956, 1964, 1972, and 1980, but I could no more duplicate those workouts than I could fly to the moon. I approached my training differently in each of those years, and I will continue to do so in the future.

Our bodies change. Our situations change. Our motivations change. Everything is different. A particular danger is for someone who starts running again after a slack period of a dozen or more years to think he can train like he did in high school. There are a lot of other things you did in high school that you wouldn't—or shouldn't—do again. Be wise.

## MAKE SMALL CHANGES

Coach Babington suggested only one small adaptation to Jennings: Increase mileage. She added only 10 to 20 miles to her weekly total. Both coach and athlete realized that if she made too radical a shift in her training routine, they risked undoing all her previous gains.

At one point in my career, I tried to increase the number of quarters in my interval workouts (going from 10 to 20) and to decrease the times (going from 70 seconds to 60). Before I could reach my goal of 20 60-second 400s, I crashed. Years later, I reflected on this training mistake with Frank McBride, who was coaching me at the time. "We violated at least two of [German coach Waldermar] Gerschler's five training principles," he admitted. (See chapter 8 for more about Gerschler and his theories on interval training.)

That's the kind of mistake you make only once if you're an intelligent runner. If you're superintelligent, you'll avoid making it even once. In plotting your training progression, concentrate on improving one area at a time—and go about it gingerly.

## GET OUT OF THE RUT

Runners often get stuck on plateaus and fail to improve because they fail to change their training. Distance running will help you run faster; so will speedwork. But if you're stuck on one type of training to the complete exclusion of all others, you probably will fail to maximize your performance. One way to improve is to do something different, almost regardless of what that something is.

Be innovative. Change training sites. Join a different fitness club. Find a coach. Shift sports. If you're a track runner, you might benefit from doing some road running. Road racers probably should move to the track—or try cross-country. There are many types of distance running, including orienteering and biathlons. If you move from one to the other, it will provide new goals, if nothing else.

## PROGRAM SOME REST

The hard/easy training pioneered by the University of Oregon's Bill Bowerman works well. By taking an easy day or two, runners can come back on their hard day and run that much harder. Ball State's Dr. David Costill claims that muscle changes occur on the rest day following a hard training session, rather than on the hard day. If you work hard day after day, you eventually tear down muscle.

Bruce Tulluh states: "Most athletes will find that two hard sessions and one race per week is as much as they can take, with the other days being easy running for recuperation."

## RESPECT YOUR ENVIRONMENT

If you wake up in the morning and find the street in front of your house covered with a sheet of ice from a freezing rain, that's probably not the day to head to the track for a workout of repeat quarters—unless that track's indoors. Obviously, everybody needs to take note of the weather for specific workouts. But the best way to prepare for weather is to do so well in advance, when you plan your schedule.

Living in the Midwest, I know that winter offers a good period for long aerobic runs, since I can run slowly while wearing several layers of clothes and picking my way across icy patches or puddles in the road. Spring is a good time for fast anaerobic runs, since the footing is good and the weather's still cool. Summer is a time for repetition running, since I can pause between fast bursts to cool down or even take a drink. But this scenario wouldn't necessarily hold true for a runner in Arizona or Alaska. In planning your training, you have to be aware of the environment in which you run.

## PROGRESS CAREFULLY TOWARD YOUR GOAL

To improve with each performance, you need to carefully and progressively adapt your training. This is the principle of overload, whose historic innovator, the ancient Greek wrestler Milo, got stronger each day by lifting onto his shoulders a calf that eventually became a bull. When we increase our mileage on a daily or weekly basis, we essentially are doing the same.

But a lot of, well, *bull* is offered to runners about how they should progress. Some theories say to increase our mileage by 10 percent a week or to run interval quarters a second faster each week. I don't believe in formulas. As you progress, make certain that you do so conservatively. But do progress.

## PUT IT IN WRITING

One way to motivate yourself is visually, with either a chart or a poster on your wall. If your goal is a specific race time, maybe you should pass those numbers every day when you go out to train.

I'm a big believer in visual aids. I designed my schedule for the present season by drawing a calendar with eight months of dates. On it, I outline in red my scheduled mileage for each week and the race dates where I want to hit my peak. The calendar hangs on the wall in my basement, where I do my stretching and weight training. I pass that chart every day when I go to run. I scribble mileage and times on it, too, in addition to recording them in my diary. That lets me know whether I'm still on schedule with my planned training.

## REVIEW REGULARLY

By reviewing my plans from time to time, I discover whether my original planning was overly optimistic. If it's April and my longest run over the past three months was 12 miles, but I plotted 18 miles for that date, I realize I may need to take a more realistic look at my plans and my goals. It may be time to return to the first tip: Plan ahead.

# Chapter 15

# SMART TRAINING

## STAY ON TRACK WHEN THE GOING GETS TOUGH

**N**ot everybody runs at the same level year after year after year. We move from peaks to valleys, gearing up for a road race, gearing down when other interests take precedence. Sometimes we become injured. Sometimes we become bored. Sometimes we quit running (or run less) rather than fight the winds of winter or the dog days of summer. Sometimes we switch sports, shifting into skiing or swimming or cycling, activities that keep us fit but do little to help us run fast. When we move back to the 5-K or 10-K, we sometimes encounter troubles.

Triathlons and biathlons have attracted many runners. Cross-training was the fitness buzzword of the 1980s. But although cross-training may maintain or even improve your aerobic power, it can develop muscles antagonistic to running. You also can get into such terrific overall shape that you push yourself into an injury when you move back to the 10-K or other road distances. That happened to me once after a winter of hard skiing. Spending a month in Europe, I went from a cross-country ski race in Norway one weekend to a road race in Italy several weeks later. I ran quite well—then limped through the rest of the spring. Since that experience, I learned to be more cautious coming back, giving my running muscles time to realign themselves.

# GETTING BACK ON TRACK

Carl Foster, Ph.D., director of cardiac rehabilitation and exercise training at Sinai-Samaritan Medical Center, warns against overconfidence bred from cross-training. "Staying active in other sports is a two-edged sword," he says. "Your cardiac output may be high if you bike or swim or ski, but your muscles and joints may not be ready for the different stresses in running. If you're in good general shape, it's too easy to overdo it. Then you're sore and creaky, and you can beat yourself up orthopedically."

The same is true after a change in goals. Runners stay sharp mentally by reevaluating goals and accepting new challenges. We add miles to finish a marathon; we add speed to run a 10-K. That keeps us motivated. But even though you already possess a strong aerobic base, you can't make a major training shift without careful thought. When increasing intensity (or mileage), you first need to move *very* slowly.

What happens to the body when we move back to the 10-K? The mind remembers those quarters run on the track that are so vital for peak performance, but maybe the body isn't ready for that level of stress. As I mentioned in chapter 14, past training diaries can be traps as well as assets in planning your first steps to coming back to that level of performance.

Complicating matters are the effects of aging: It is easier to resume fast training in your 20s or 30s than in your 40s and 50s. And beyond 60, some scientists suggest walking may be all the aerobic exercise we need. Of course, another factor is how long you have been away from running.

# HERE TODAY, GONE TOMORROW

Scientists now can describe the effects of detraining, or how quickly we go out of shape. At the University of Texas at Austin, Edward F. Coyle, Ph.D., convinced a group of highly trained runners (who ran 80 miles a week) and cyclists (who rode 250 miles a week) to quit training. Their measured oxygen uptake scores declined rapidly at first, then less so. The best trained, those who had worked hardest to get in shape, lost the most. Those less trained had less to lose. Dr. Coyle determined that athletes lost half their aerobic fitness within 12 to 21 days, then half of their remaining fitness level within the next 12- to 21-day period, and so on. By three months, all were detrained.

## ONE WEEK OFF, TWO WEEKS TO COME BACK

Scientists find it more difficult to measure *retraining*, how long it takes to get *back* in shape. "There's very little data," concedes the University of Florida's Dr. Michael L. Pollock. Nevertheless, scientists can make some educated guesses. Dr. Coyle suggests that every week lost requires two weeks spent in recovery. Ball State researcher Dr. David Costill estimates that you can regain aerobic fitness within four to eight weeks. "Strength changes take longer," he claims.

Strength, of course, equals speed. It will take you longer to regain your ability to run fast than your ability to run far.

This is why layoffs trouble many runners. As a high school coach, I was asked by one of my students how much she lost by taking the week off between Christmas and New Year's. Citing Dr. Coyle, I told her that she would need two weeks to get back to where she was previously.

Most scientists believe that people with previous conditioning can regain their speed sooner than people starting from scratch. In other words, a born-again runner has an advantage over one who never started. "The muscles may have some memory," muses Dr. Costill, "or maybe we're smarter with our training the second time." Dr. Costill's colleague William Fink adds: "A lot depends on how far you've gotten out of shape. There comes a point where you've lost everything, when starting over means truly starting from scratch."

## SOME TRAINING QUALITIES VANISH, SOME REMAIN

The very best athletes find it most difficult to regain past peaks. When you're at the elite level, improvements of a few seconds require herculean efforts involving months, maybe years, of hard training. At that level, you can't afford time off; it's too difficult to reclimb the mountain. Alberto Salazar was America's top marathoner between the 1980 and 1984 Olympics, setting records at the Boston and New York City Marathons and running 10-K times well under 28 minutes. In 1990, Salazar attempted a comeback, which he abandoned when he was unable to break 29 minutes. Salazar remained in excellent physical shape; he simply lost his speed.

In Dr. Coyle's detraining studies, he identified one reason for the immediate fitness decline—loss of blood volume. During the first 12 to 21 days away from training, you lose as much as half a quart (500 milliliters) of blood. Dr. Coyle states: "Previously, researchers thought detraining was because of deterioration of the heart. Actually, the heart had less blood to pump to the muscles."

When you retrain, you *regain* that lost blood volume. It's a natural form of blood-doping. Not only can you transport oxygen to the muscles more efficiently again, but you also have more fluid available for sweating, which helps cool your body. For this reason, you are better off resuming training during the cool days of spring rather than waiting for summer, when your body may not be acclimatized to the heat. Dr. Coyle says runners can regain plasma blood volume within a week, although reproduction of red blood cells takes longer.

Not all training benefits vanish during long layoffs. Fast-twitch muscles hold some of their endurance. Muscle capillaries, which increase by 40 to 50 percent during training, remain and retain their ability to eliminate the waste products of exercise, such as lactic acid.

But not all systems of the body detrain or retrain equally. Your skeletal system, for instance, may not accept the strain of training at your previous level, particularly as you age. Remember, a runner who loses six years of training must also cope with six years of normal aging.

# *TRAIN SMARTER*

Kenneth E. Sparks, Ph.D., director of clinical program development for St. Vincent Charity Hospital in Cleveland and member of a world-record 2-mile relay team in his 20s, resumed hard training as he approached age 40. He returned to a fast 4:16 mile and 2:39:00 marathon, but he also needed surgery after injuring an Achilles tendon. "If you've been a competitor in the past, you're used to training on the edge," says Dr. Sparks. "This may be all right when you're young, when you heal rapidly. As you age, you need to train smarter and be more in tune with your body. Every time you go out to run, it could be your last workout, because of an injury."

Runners who return inevitably experience sore muscles, but not because of lactic acid, which is often identified as a culprit. According to Frederick C. Hagerman of Ohio University's Department of Zoological and Biomedical Sciences, the body can rapidly remetabolize the lactic acid that pools in muscles during hard exercise. More of a problem is caused by different motor patterns. Dr. Costill agrees. "You're not used to coordinating the new activity," he explains. "After you've practiced it several times, your muscles discover the right motor patterns, and you won't get sore."

For this reason, a born-again runner should not face muscles as sore as when he first learned to run, assuming he is conservative in his retraining. According to James D. Richardson of Miami-Dade Community College's physical education department: "Most muscle soreness is temporary and apparently has no negative, long-term effect."

Retraining for the 10-K need not be that difficult. And it is certainly easier than starting to run for the first time. Remember the fun it once was to run fast? Remember the good feeling of wind in your hair? If you are returning to short-distance events after being away for whatever reason, the following tips may make your journey back more pleasant.

**Have a goal in mind.** A goal may be as simple as going out to do your first run. Ask yourself, why do I want to run again? To get in shape? To improve my previous times? To compete in some race? Plan your training well ahead so as to achieve that goal.

**Consider how long you've been gone.** Depending upon your time away from fast training, you will have an easy or hard time coming back. Expect to spend at least two days getting back in shape for every day lost.

**Forget the past.** Workouts done years ago bear no relevance to what you can do today—and can be a cause of injury if you try to duplicate them without your past level of fitness. Once you regain your base fitness, you can ask yourself whether you want to (or can) resume old training patterns, including speedwork.

**Decide if you can do it better this time.** In your previous life as a runner, did you make mistakes that can be avoided this time? Reevaluate your entire approach to training. Don't get trapped in old training habits that maybe didn't produce the best results.

**Consider your age.** Runners in their 20s can head back to the track after layoffs as though they never took any time off. It becomes progressively difficult to regain lost speed once into your 30s, 40s, 50s, and beyond. But it's not impossible. Use techniques such as stretching and creative rest that you might have ignored previously.

**Embrace speedwork cautiously.** Some speedwork seems necessary to regain peak performance. But until you rebuild your aerobic base, workouts that are too intense may cause excessive fatigue and discourage you. Even with that base built, your tendons and ligaments may not support the power developed by your lungs and muscles.

**Recognize that strength returns slowest.** Just as strength is slowest to fade when you stop running, it takes longest to return. Strength also equals speed. You will find it toughest to regain the top end of your conditioning, even when you're back in reasonably good shape.

**Don't race too soon.** Competition can be a good way to measure your speed, but you risk injury by going too hard. It also takes time away from training. Go into early races with a relaxed mood, and don't worry about fast times.

**Be cautious.** If previously injured, you should be particularly cautious. One important question to ask: "Have I determined the cause of the injury?" Rest is sometimes not enough. You may reinjure yourself if you train at your previous level.

**Keep the faith.** At times, it may seem the road back is too long to travel. But you *can* move back to road racing and perform at a high level. All it takes is discipline and patience.

# Chapter *16*

# *MARATHONERS ONLY*

## *WHAT YOU NEED TO KNOW ABOUT SHORT RUNS*

**J**ulie Isphording expresses dismay that she doesn't run faster in 10-K races. "Regardless of the distance, I just settle into my marathon pace," sighs Isphording, who ran the marathon for the United States in the 1984 Olympics and has a personal record of 2:30:54.

She concedes that one reason for her lack of race speed is that she never trains for shorter distances. "I don't like the track," says Isphording, "but I love endurance, so I always fall back on what feels most comfortable."

Of course, that's one of the major reasons why runners fail to run fast. As Indiana University track coach Sam Bell says: "You don't learn to run fast by running slow."

If your goal is fast times in the marathon, you can be

excused for focusing your attention on endurance rather than speed. A lot of beginners who move up to the 10-K keep going until they reach the marathon. They just continue to gradually increase their mileage until that glorious moment when they cross the finish line of their first 26-mile, 385-yard race. It's a moment not to be denied.

The training necessary for reaching a marathon finish line is relatively simple. You go just a bit farther every week. You focus on endurance, not speed. You need not worry about bounding or fartlek or interval training, the fine-tuning necessary for running fast. But after running a few marathons and seeing their times plateau, runners sometimes look back and wonder if they may have missed something along the way. They did: the opportunity to improve their short-distance speed.

That's not a major oversight. The opportunity remains. However, when it comes time to move *down* to the 10-K, you need to rethink your approach to training. The same is true when you return to the 10-K after a layoff or an injury. Let's discuss the approaches you might take.

## GETTING READY FOR THE CHALLENGE

Wendell Miller, an investment consultant from Lake Bluff, Illinois, notes that many of his friends have become disenchanted with marathons. "They're moving down to shorter distances," says Miller. "They don't want to spend three or four weeks recovering after each race."

Don Kardong, who finished fourth in the 1976 Olympic marathon, has refocused his goals on shorter distances. "I don't have the time to prepare adequately for the marathon," says Kardong, "so I'm refocusing my training to regain leg speed."

But Kardong notes that not all runners want to make this training shift, whether or not they continue to run marathon distances. "They're hooked on the pleasure of going out for a long run at a steady speed," he says. "They don't want to give that up."

Another factor that may influence your training is the fear of injury from too much hard or fast training. If you possess more endurance than speed, you also may naturally gravitate to the type of training you do best—running long and easy—whether or not you race long distances.

It is a matter of genetic fact that some athletes are blessed with more strength and/or speed than others. If you want success as an athlete, goes one adage, choose your parents carefully. Genetics are an important factor in athletic success. Three genetic factors most influence your basic speed.

**Fiber type:** Muscles have two basic fiber types: fast-twitch and slow-twitch. The former are good for quick bursts of energy. They rapidly burn stored glycogen in the muscle and function well anaerobically, without oxygen. Anaerobic metabolism, however, is inefficient for distance events. Fast-twitch fibers fatigue rapidly.

Slow-twitch muscles contract more slowly but maintain their contractions longer. They are fueled aerobically, with oxygen, and work well during distance events.

Most people have a balance of fast-twitch and slow-twitch muscles. A few have a preponderance of one or the other, which contributes to their success in specific events.

**Neurological patterns:** Another word for this is *reflexes*. These are the impulses transmitted from the brain to the muscles. Normally, the slow-twitch fibers in any given muscle are recruited before the fast-twitch fibers. Athletes with better reflexes are able to activate the latter more quickly.

**Biomechanics:** This relates to your body type and how the various parts of your body fit together and move together. The length of your legs dictates how much ground you cover with each stride, an essential for running fast. Your footplant may determine whether you can resist injury. Even as gifted a runner as two-time Olympic champion Sebastian Coe wore orthotics toward the end of his career.

When I first began coaching at the local high school and running daily with the team, one of the seniors on the team, a 6-footer, impressed me with his strength and endurance. Only at the first track meet of the season, when I watched him run 3200 meters from the top row of the stadium, did I realize that he had the legs of someone 5 feet 6 inches tall and the trunk of someone 6 feet 6 inches tall. His biomechanical configuration obviously limited his ability as a runner.

Ball State researcher Dr. David Costill has a word for such individuals. Dr. Costill calls them genetically "cursed," noting that they never will be able to achieve complete athletic success because they lack the true talent of the natural athlete. Dr. Costill himself was cursed as a runner. Despite considerable effort training for the marathon, his best times were well over 3 hours. When he returned to swimming, a sport in which he had success in college, he won numerous masters championships.

"People who succeed in the extreme events—the 100 meters and the marathon—are very clearly of two different genetic types," says Dr. Costill. "But most events fall in the middle. They require endurance *and* speed. So it's not surprising that among people who succeed in a given sport, some have more slow-twitch muscles and others have more fast-twitch muscles. They're all in the same sport, and they're equally good. They fall into that middle zone, where combinations of strength and endurance come together. This is where intelligent and specific training can have a major effect on whether you succeed or fail."

# SEARCHING FOR SPEED

Regardless of your genetic assets or liabilities, you can improve relative to your own personal ability. If you are an endurance-endowed marathoner moving down to the 10-K (and distances below), here are some tips to help you in your search for speed.

**Shorten your long runs.** Typically, runners in marathon training do a weekly long, easy run, often on Sunday mornings. They usually run about 20 miles, a distance that takes most runners 2 to 3 hours to cover at somewhere between a 6- and 9-minute pace. Olympic marathoner Benji Durden, who now coaches runners of various abilities in Boulder, Colorado, suggests placing a cap on Sunday training at 2 hours, keeping the mileage down to 15 or less. "Along with that cap comes an increase in tempo," Durden advises. "People need to pick up the pace in their long runs."

**Cut your weekly mileage.** The more miles you run each week, the slower those miles must be. By cutting mileage, you permit yourself to train at a faster tempo. You can run fresh and run fast. There are two ways to cut mileage: One is to cut the distance of each daily run; the other is to plan more rest days.

**Race at shorter distances.** "Marathoners tend to run a lot of 10-K races," says Durden. "If your goal race is that distance, you need to compete at still shorter distances." Participating in 5-K races will help improve your speed. Also, consider a move to the track to run 1500- and 3000-meter races.

**Move down in distance gingerly.** If you suddenly switch to 800-meter races on the track, you raise the risk of injury. Remember, your body is not accustomed to sudden bursts of speed. So be cautious in both your training and your racing at your new-found pace.

**Shift the focus of your training.** Instead of doing speed training one day a week and tempo training another, shift to two speed days. When marathoners do interval training, they often do long repeats, up to 1 mile. For shorter races, you need to do shorter repeats, like 200 and 400 meters.

**Reintroduce yourself to the track.** To get yourself into the mood for running fast, hang out where the sprinters train. You don't need to use starting blocks, but workouts where you can accurately monitor your speed with a stopwatch over precisely measured distances can reintroduce you to the concept and feel of running fast.

**Set realistic goals.** Don't believe computer charts that suggest if you ran your last marathon in under 3 hours, you can do a 5:10 mile. Such charts don't account for the fact that you may have more slow-twitch than fast-twitch fibers. Set realistic short-term goals. Echoing Yogi Berra, Durden says: "If you get there, you get there."

# *EPILOGUE*

On a sunny Saturday in July 1991, I jogged through the streets of Turku, Finland, crossed the river, and headed up the stadium road to the site of the World Veterans Championships, in which I was scheduled to compete. As I turned onto the stadium road, I passed the statue of Paavo Nurmi, arguably the world's greatest distance runner.

It cast a shadow in my path, a reflection of times past.

Turku was once Nurmi's home. In a career spanning three Olympic Games, Nurmi—in what must be considered the ultimate example of how to run fast—won seven gold and three silver medals. His brightest moment came at the 1924 Games, where he won the 1500 and 5000 meters within a span of 2 hours.

I never raced Nurmi because he was a generation before my time. But I raced his son in 1956, on the same Turku track that I had come to race on for the 1991 World Vets. At the time, I was competing on a U.S. team traveling through Finland. The experience was educational, to say the least. On our way to Turku, our team raced in three smaller towns. I scored a victory in each at distances between 3000 and 5000 meters. My head swelled with pride. This was Finland, home of great distance runners, where Americans were not expected to succeed.

But then we arrived in Turku, the big league. It was like an entire baseball team moving from the minors to the majors. On the last lap of a 3000-meter race, two Finns swept past, beating me to the finish. One was Nurmi's son, a shadow of his father but still good. The next day, I took another third in a 3000-meter steeplechase race. Afterward, I sat in a trackside sauna, my disappointment in defeat balanced only by my having finished at least close to a legend.

## *A RETURN FOR GLORY*

Turku in 1991 became a passage back to youth, a quest for lost glory. In today's run-for-pay era, Turku has drifted into a backwater of international athletic competition. But its track once was the world's fastest. John Landy set a world record there. So did Emil Zatopek and Ron Clarke.

Jogging past Paavo Nurmi's statue, I couldn't help but reflect on those greats—that here I was, still following in their footsteps. Nurmi's statue guards the approach to the track, which sits atop a rocky hill. It is surrounded by a sawdust jogging trail used in the winters for cross-country skiing. There is a separate area with a straightaway used only for warm-up.

I sat stretching in this area, reflecting upon the single-minded effort that had brought me to this moment. For nearly two years—a time that coincided with the writing of this book—I had plotted my return. Just before coming to Turku, I turned 60, which moved me into a new age category. It's easier to win when you're the youngest old guy in your race. Still, the competition was tough. Five thousand dynamic, well-conditioned athletes were entered in competition. "If I want to succeed," I told myself, "I *must* be at my very best."

In the months before the event, I had trained hard. I spent the winter building an aerobic base, following a training program similar to the one I present in this book. In the spring, I worked on my speed endurance with sharp runs near race pace. In summer, I switched to sprints and strides and went to the local track regularly to work on barrier technique. I practiced dynamic flexibility. I stretched. I obtained regular massages, pampering my mind as well as my body. I tapered carefully to assure going to the line strong.

## THE SHOWDOWN

Twenty-one runners lined up for the 2000-meter steeple-chase for men 60 to 64 years of age—remarkable when you consider the difficulty of the event. It requires leaping over five barriers, including a water jump, in each lap. I drew lane 21, which forced me to start my race off the track.

The early pace seemed too swift. I dawdled midpack, fearful that my medal quest was futile. But those ahead began faltering. With 500 meters to go, I moved into third. I wondered if I was doomed to finish this Turku race in third—again.

But then my body took control over my brain; I found myself suddenly young again. My stride stretched. I flew over the barriers. A runner appeared in front of me; I passed. And then another runner; I sprinted by. I won!

My wife said later that I acted shamelessly. I crossed the line with my arms spread wide, like Carl Lewis. I bent down and kissed the track, like I once had seen an Italian steeplechaser do at the Olympics. I took a victory lap, although nobody had requested I do so—and few were in the stands to cheer. (It is one of the prerogatives of old age to act crazy now and then.)

I still do not deserve to tie the shoelaces of the great Paavo Nurmi, but at least I'm not running in his shadow anymore.

I've taught myself to run fast.

# *ACKNOWLEDGMENTS*

If you benefit from reading this book—if you indeed learn how to run fast—you must join me in thanking those individuals without whose help its publication would have been impossible.

The ones deserving the most praise are those who offered the information that provides the book's backbone: the scientists, coaches, and runners who have willingly shared their expertise and experiences. Their names and titles pepper the pages of the book. To repeat them all would, unfortunately, offer an indigestible list. So to those whose thoughts and ideas have become an important part of *Run Fast,* I offer the joint thanks of runners everywhere.

Several individuals deserve extra praise. Whenever I need an expert opinion, I usually turn first to my friend Dr. Dave Costill at Ball State University. To assure the accuracy of the book, I wanted someone to "vette" the manuscript. Dave introduced me to Dawn E. Anderson, a doctoral student at his Human Performance Laboratory. Dawn read the book carefully and offered important suggestions.

For a coach's point of view, I turned to another close friend: Steve Kearney, a track and cross-country coach at Chesterton High School, near my home. For a runner's viewpoint, I used my son Kevin, who ran on two Big Ten championship teams while at Indiana University. Steve and Kevin helped steer me straight.

My wife, Rose, serves as a sounding board for my writing and accompanies me to races, tolerating my hubris in victory, my despair in defeat. I also must mention our other two grown children: David (senior editor for *Tennis* magazine) and Laura Sandall (public relations manager for Marshall Field's).

In teaching you how to run fast, I share some personal experiences that I've written about before in magazines. Three editors in particular have been involved in assigning running articles to me: Joe Henderson from the early days of *Runner's World,* Marc Bloom from *The Runner,* and

Amby Burfoot of the current *Runner's World,* now published by Rodale Press.

Researching a book for Rodale Press is easy because of the company's excellent research library in Emmaus, Pennsylvania. Assistant librarian Evangeline Bicknell aided me in my search for published information on running, as did Janet Glassman.

Just as it is helpful for a runner to have a good coach, it is helpful for an author to have good editors. Rodale Press's Sharon Faelten helped get the book started, and Kathleen Becker edited the manuscript. Angela Miller, my agent in New York City, encouraged the project and supervised its business aspects.

Also a word about Robert Rodale, who died in an automobile accident in Moscow as I was preparing this book. I met Bob only once, having had breakfast with him and Amby Burfoot in Boston before the marathon. He impressed me as a quiet, sincere, likable man. I would have enjoyed knowing Bob better, because his belief that good health comes from many directions made this book possible.

Should you improve as a runner as a result of reading *Run Fast,* it will be impossible to say that this or that person carved $3/10$ second off your 10-K time. They are all responsible and deserve our appreciation.

# RECOMMENDED READING

### Dynamic Flexibility

Higdon, Kevin. "Bound to Help." *The Runner*, September 1982.

Radcliffe, James C., and Robert C. Farentinos. *Plyometrics: Explosive Power Training*. Champaign, Illinois: Human Kinetics Publishers, Inc., 1985.

### Fartlek

Dellinger, Bill (with Bob Wischnia). "Fartlek Training." *Runner's World*, January 1981.

Holmer, Gosta. "Fartlek." *Track & Field News*, April 1949.

Noden, Merrill. "Playing on the Run." *The Runner*, August 1985.

O'Connor, W. H. "Distance Training With Controlled Fartlek." *Scholastic Coach*, March 1978.

### Hill Training

Glover, Bob. "Hill Training." *Running & Fitness*, May–June 1982.

### Interval Training

Daniels, Jack. "Cruise Control." *Runner's World*, June 1990.

———. "Interval Training and Performance." *Sports Medicine*, July–August 1984.

Dellinger, Bill (with Bob Wischnia). "Interval Training." *Runner's World*, March 1981.

Ecker, Tom. "Progressive Interval Training." *The Athletic Journal*, April 1977.

Galloway, Jeff. "Safe Speed." *Runner's World*, June 1988.

Kaufmann, Elizabeth. "The New Rhythms of Fitness." *American Health*, December 1989.

Lamb, David R. "Understanding Intervals." *Runner's World,* June 1986.

Mitchell, Brian. "The Case for Interval Training." *Athletics Weekly,* 13 January 1979.

Powers, Scotty K. "Principles of Interval Training." *Track Technique,* Winter 1978.

Ragg, Kerry E. "Continuous and Interval Training Program Influences on Leg Speed." *Journal of Sports Medicine & Physical Fitness,* June 1979.

## Running Form

Anderson, Owen. "Economics 101." *Runner's World,* November 1990.

Armstrong, Lawrence E. "Biomechanical Changes in Selected Collegiate Sprinters Due to Increased Velocity." *Track and Field Quarterly,* Summer 1983.

Conley, Douglas L. "Training for Aerobic Capacity and Running Economy." *The Physician and Sportsmedicine,* April 1981.

## Self-Coaching

Anderson, Bob. *Stretching.* Bolinas, California: Shelter Publications, 1980. (Available from Bob Anderson, Box 767, Palmer Lakes, CO 80133; (800) 333–1307.)

Anderson, Owen. "The 10 Km Commandments." *Running* (United Kingdom), July 1990. (First published in *Running Research News,* November–December 1989.)

———. "Should You Run Fast During Your Taper?" *Running Research News,* July–August 1990.

———. "Mammoth Mileage Not Mandatory for Magnificent Miles." *Running Research News,* May–June 1990.

Dellinger, Bill (with Bob Wischnia). "What Distance Runners Learn from Sprinters." *Runner's World,* June 1982.

Fleck, Steven J., and William J. Kraemer. *Designing Resistance Training Programs.* Champaign, Illinois: Human Kinetics Books, 1987.

Higdon, Hal. "The Spirit That Moves Us." *The Runner,* September 1982.

Humphreys, John, and Ron Holman. *Focus on Middle-Distance Running.* London: Adam & Charles Black, 1985.

Janssen, Peter G. J. M. *Training Lactate Pulse-Rate.* Finland: Polar Electro Oy, 1987. (Available from Polar USA, Inc.; (203) 359–1966.)

Smith, Paul A. "Training the Middle Distance Runner." *The Athletic Journal,* April 1981.

Tulloh, Bruce. "Tulloh's Guide to the Famous Five." *Running* (United Kingdom), August 1990.

Yakimov, A. "Middle and Long Distance Training Methods." *Track Technique,* Spring 1981.

## Speedwork

Boggis, Donald E., Jr. "Improve Your Running Events." *The Athletic Journal,* January 1984.

Galloway, Jeff. "Speed Work, and Play." *The Runner,* October 1983.

Glover, Bob. "Easing into Speed Training." *Runner's World,* August 1986.

Shyne, Kevin. "Speed." *Esquire,* February 1984.

## Strength Training

Stone, Michael H., and Harold S. O'Brien. *Weight Training: A Scientific Approach.* Edina, Minnesota: Burgess International Group, Inc., 1987.

Note: Page references in *italic* indicate tables.